Known

DISCOVERING YOUR
IDENTITY AND WORTH IN GOD

Known

AN
INTERACTIVE
JOURNEY

PHILIPPA HANNA

etc Equipping
the Church

This book is dedicated to my little girl Ozma. Sweet Ozma, you are loved beyond measure. You are my greatest purpose and the love of my life. May you grow up knowing your value, seeing your beauty and believing in your boundless potential.

Love Mummy x

Contents

Introduction

> You have searched me, LORD,
> and you know me.
>
> PSALM 139:1

Wouldn't it be great to feel truly seen, heard and appreciated? How fabulous would it be to wake up each morning empowered and fearless, not worrying what others will think of you? **What would you give to feel secure and at peace with your God-given identity?**

Perhaps you already feel that you know and love who you are. Maybe you're well and truly 'happy in your skin'. But chances are, like most of us you are on a journey with that. You're probably still figuring out what you believe, what you want out of life and how you 'identify'. If you feel like a work in progress, don't worry—this is the perfect book for you. However you feel about your identity, the good news is you can feel better. Whether you're in a positive and confident place, or feeling low and insecure, there are things you can do to reach a deeper level of peace with who you

9

are. It is possible to live a life where you feel **known**, **loved** and **secure**. That is what this journal is designed to help you with.

We are about to go on a journey of self-discovery. Our goal will be to move closer to a place of security in who God created us to be. Hopefully, in time, we can step fully into that God-given identity. By moving through this creative, guided process, together we can begin to discover the depth of God's love for us, as well as the true beauty and value of who we are.

How to use this journal

We all want to be our true and best selves. This journal is designed to be an interactive companion for you. It's all yours, for your own enjoyment and expression. It's a safe place to record and reflect on how you feel. You don't ever need to share it with anyone, so be as open as you like! We will be exploring some of the key building blocks of identity. Our aim will be to look at ourselves honestly, celebrating our strengths and quirks. We can also be real about our weaknesses and find ways to grow.

Each section has different components that look a bit like this:

 Getting to properly know ourselves often means stripping away some uncomfortable layers. Every section of this journal has an 'Honesty First' feature. This is where we will get as real as possible. If you need to, take a deep breath before you write or doodle and ask God to help you be **your most unfiltered self**. Or, if you prefer, make your response quickly before doubt gets in the way! Whatever you do, try to be authentic, because that will serve you best.

Being authentic is not always easy. It's often simpler to go with the flow or borrow opinions from other people. But Scripture tells us *'the truth will set you free'*. If we want to live in freedom, we must first be **truthful**, even if that means expressing confusion, doubt or fear.

Sometimes our surroundings make it hard for us to open up. For example, if we're surrounded by people who always seem upbeat, admitting we're feeling low or discouraged can be tough. If we are surrounded by people who seem to have unshakeable faith, it might be hard to admit we're struggling to believe. But until we're willing to be fully honest with ourselves, there's not much chance we can ever *be* ourselves around others. However uncomfortable, telling the truth is vital for our sense of identity.

After 'Honesty First', we will take a look at what God has to say about things. Biblical Scripture is packed full of truth, wisdom and practical advice so wisdom and practical advice so  this part is super useful. You might also find Scripture dotted around in the other sections, because it comes in handy everywhere. Even if you're still on a journey with what you believe about God, I know you'll be blown away by what Scripture has to offer. It stands the test of time and gives millions of people strength, comfort and guidance every day.

Before I had Christian faith, prayer was something I'd only ever seen on TV and experienced in school assemblies. But prayer has become extremely important for me. It's something I've learned to do throughout each day to manage anxiety and focus my mind. Lots of people use meditation in a similar way. For me, prayer is more powerful because it takes the focus away from my weakness and onto God's power. Whether you're new to prayer or a fully fledged prayer warrior, it offers a chance to bring all the pieces of yourself to God, or even just to see things in a fresh light. There's no harm in giving it a shot.

Testimony is powerful! So now and again I'll share a little story time with you to help unpack the section. The stories might be my

own or borrowed from others I've encountered across my life and travels. Hopefully they will help you reflect on your own story.

Reflect and Reframe

We will also use '*Reframing*' and '*Reflecting*' within each section. Reframing is when we take something like a feeling, a memory or a recurring thought and choose to think of it in a more helpful way. In effect, we are **choosing to tell our story differently**. This will help us build a healthier view of who we are. For example, if we have discovered that our self-image is not great, we might attempt to frame our thoughts more positively by saying things like, *'I'm learning to see myself as God sees me'*.

Section One

A first look at who we are

Before we get into the full flow of the journal, let's practise the process by taking a quick look at how we feel about ourselves right now. Using the following scales, circle, scribble or colour around the number that represents how you're feeling. You don't have to pick an exact number; a vague position will do. There is no right or wrong response and no one is testing you. This is just to help you get a clearer picture of where you are today. We will come back to it later on.

Feel free to be creative, scribbling, adding notes and your own thoughts around the scales.

Do you feel you know who you are?

No idea   Figuring it out   I know myself inside out!

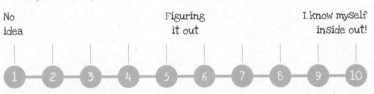

How do you feel about yourself in general?

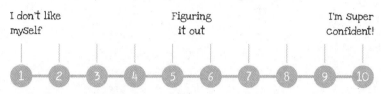

| I don't like myself | | | Figuring it out | | | | I'm super confident! |

How do you feel about your physical appearance?

| I hate the way I look | | | I accept the way I look | | | | I'm simply fabulous! |

How do you feel about your future?

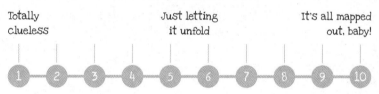

| Totally clueless | | | Just letting it unfold | | | | It's all mapped out, baby! |

What about your gifts and talents?

| I'm not good at anything | | | I have potential | | | | Gifted and talented! |

And how are the relationships in your life?

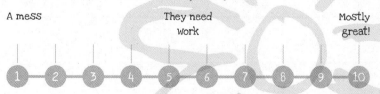

| A mess | | | They need work | | | | Mostly great! |

Now you've done some scribbling and circling, take a moment to pray about what emerges. Does anything stand out to you? Does anything surprise or concern you? We all have some work to do in these areas, but if anything strikes you as an area for growth, it's time to bring it to God. Say this prayer with me:

God, I know I need help in some of these areas. I want to get to a place where I know and love myself fully. Help me not to worry about what I'm feeling, but simply to look at it, accept it and move on to the next phase. I release it all to You now. Amen.

If something is burning in your heart after considering these things, take a few moments to jot some notes down about it. Try to be positive because there are always ways to improve things and, with God's help, we can certainly grow.

....

....

....

What is 'identity'?

> So God created mankind in his own image, in the image of God he created them;
>
> GENESIS 1:27

Before we go any further, it's probably helpful if we clarify what we mean when we use the word '**identity**'. Lots of people talk about the way they identify in the 21st century. Some will relate this to gender, culture, sexuality or race. But these are essentially 'group identities'. When we identify in these ways, we are actually defining ourselves by the groups we belong to. There is so much more for us to discover!

It isn't surprising that we identify into groups because to some degree it simplifies things. Dividing people into neat categories based on variables like race, religion and sexuality helps make sense of the world we live in. But when it comes to our identity in God there are two truths we need to grasp.

The first is that **identity is individual**. Just as no two snowflakes or fingerprints are identical, no two people are either. Being part of a group can mean a lot to us. We often find a sense of belonging and community within a group, which we need. Groups can also help us to learn about our heritage or history. But every group is made up of individuals who don't all look or think exactly the same way. For example, you may identify strongly as a girl, but not all girls are the same. You may identify strongly within your race community too, but not everyone within your community thinks exactly the way you do. So, when we're building a confident picture of who we are in God, we have to dig a little deeper than the boxes we fit into and step into our individual identity.

Every person has a unique set of ideas, beliefs, gifts and experiences to add to the melting pot of life. If you like, groups reflect only primary colours; it's individuals who form all the shades within the spectrum. Instead of just blending into groups, we need to **uncover** and **illuminate** our own true colours so we can paint the world.

The second important truth about identity is that we are all created to be part of **one** group: **God's family**. Your colour, passion and beauty have a place within it. Your ideas are needed. You were designed with all your unique qualities to take your place there and shine. Uncovering, embracing and stepping fully into who we are helps us see where we fit in the bigger picture.

Cutting through the noise

We're faced with a daily stream of information about who we are supposed to be. Social media is full of perfect-looking people 'living their best lives' in an air-brushed world. This constant exposure to what looks perfect can leave us feeling confused, insecure and unfulfilled. We can end up setting a bunch of body, relationship, career and 'squad' goals we're not even sure we need.

On top of that, the world seems to be getting spiritually and socially more complex every day. Sandwiched between glamorous images of influencers and celebs are countless political messages too. Everywhere you turn there are activists and causes. Between riots, rallies and fundraisers, our attention is being grabbed from all angles. Our hearts are tugged in a dozen directions as we try to determine what really matters to us. And all this noise is affecting our sense of identity.

In this journal, we are going to focus our attention on both what feels natural to us and who God says we are in Scripture. We will look into society's definitions too, picking apart some of the less helpful stuff. The destination we're heading for? A more peaceful and balanced view of ourselves based in God's truth.

The dictionary definition of 'identity' is:

> *the characteristics determining who or what a person or thing is.*[1]

The social science definition of 'identity' is:

> *the qualities, beliefs, personality, looks and/or expressions that make a person.*[2]

In simple terms, identity is another way of describing who we are. I could say 'I am British', for instance, or 'I am a woman'. But so many of these variables are just boxes we tick on a form. In reality, who we are goes much deeper.

To know the deeper you and the greater truth that follows the words *'I am'*, we have to begin looking at ourselves through God's eyes. Our faith gives us the *'I am'* beyond the obvious labels or boxes on forms.

Our physical attributes, beliefs, values, passions and talents are all things that differ from person to person, just the way God intended. But there are also truths about who we are that go beyond such things. Scripture helps us dig into the deeper layers of who we are as children of God.

Before we move on, let's take a moment to jot down some thoughts about ourselves. Taking a pen, pencil or coloured pens, draw or write down one thing that makes you unique. Do you have any distinguishing physical features? Do you have any interesting abilities? Remember, at this stage you don't have to like or be comfortable with these things. Just start by seeing them.

Looking at what you've drawn or written above, how do you feel? Are your thoughts positive or negative? Circle, scribble or colour on the scale below:

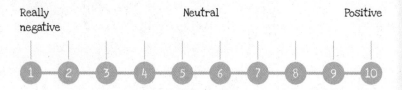

Really negative   Neutral   Positive

1 — 2 — 3 — 4 — 5 — 6 — 7 — 8 — 9 — 10

As we begin our journey, let's gather up all the pieces of how we feel and ask God to give us His perspective. You can use your own words or read the prayer below as a guide.

God, thank You for the person You've made me to be. Even though I might not always appreciate myself fully, I know there is no one else like me in this world. As I begin this journey, help me to see that You created me and love me. If there are things about myself I don't like, help me to see them in a more positive light. If it's all I can manage, let me start by just reframing one negative thought today. Amen.

Reframe

Time to start working on that reframing skill! Is there something about yourself that you constantly think about changing? If so, take a moment to 'reframe' that thing more positively in the space over the page. For example, if you have a scar that bothers you, you could reframe it like this:

I haven't always liked this scar, but it gives me a story to tell. It shows that I have been through something, felt pain and survived.

Reframe here:

....

....

....

....

....

....

....

....

....

....

....

....

....

....

Now we've practised '*Reframing*', we can park all these thoughts and move swiftly on to Section Two: **Beliefs**.

Section Two

Beliefs
What we believe about God, ourselves and others

> Set your minds on things above, not on earthly things.
>
> COLOSSIANS 3:2

Our beliefs have a profound impact on who we are. Throughout this section we will ask ourselves what we **believe** and figure out why it matters. We will give ourselves space to ask important questions like: *'Do I have doubts about God?'*, *'Could what I believe about myself affect my future?'* and *'Are my beliefs about others affecting my relationships?'*. We will address these beliefs and give ourselves permission for them to improve.

It's okay if you don't yet know what you believe about God. There's lots of pressure in society to shout about what you believe. Social media has become a real battle ground over divisive topics, with many people voicing their opinions. But there are just as many silent onlookers who aren't sure where they stand and feel afraid to join the conversation. We might feel nervous to say what we *really* think in case it isn't the popular opinion and we get 'cancelled'.

For those of us who believe in God it can be especially hard to be honest about our tussles with faith. No one wants to admit they are confused, struggling to believe or even angry at God. If you come from a Christian family, it might feel impossible to admit you have doubts. **But it's okay to feel what you're feeling.** To doubt is human. If God really is who Scripture says He is, He is big enough to handle it! He can deal with all the questions, tears and anger you can throw at Him. So, if you're holding on to something in your heart towards God at the moment, this could be the perfect time to let it out. Expressing the truth of how we feel can help bring down walls we have built inside and even begin the healing process.

In a moment, start to write some notes about what you believe right now. Try not to overthink; just scribble down whatever comes to mind. Remember, there is no way to fail or answer wrongly as this is not a test. This exercise is simply about exploration, so be as open as you can. The fact is, we are all learning and our beliefs are under construction every day. So if you don't know what you think or believe, it's okay to say so. Being truthful will help you form real opinions that actually reflect your heart.

**Write the date at the top of this section, just to remind yourself

Date:

where you were in time when you felt this way. **

Now, Write some notes below about what you believe about God. For example:

> *I believe God hears prayers, I don't believe God cares* or *I believe God always chooses others over me.*

Write some notes on your beliefs about yourself. For example:

> *I believe I have potential, I believe I am failing* or *I believe I am clumsy.*

Write some notes on your beliefs about others. For example:

I believe most people are good-natured, I believe most people can't be trusted or *I believe others will eventually let me down.*

Reflect

How was that? Did you feel you could be honest? Remember, this is a totally safe space to be open. No one is scoring or judging you. If you struggled, don't worry. We can always come back to it.

Take a moment to breathe and clear your head. Perhaps have a look out of the window or go for a little walk. When you have a moment, look back over your notes. What do you feel about the beliefs you wrote down? Are you sad, happy or confused about the way you feel? Are there things you would like to change? What we believe shapes everything in our lives. It affects the choices we make and the way we behave. But Scripture says we can be transformed by the renewing of our minds. Why not grab some coloured pencils and do some shading over or around your notes. If there is a belief that makes you sad, maybe colour it blue. If you have a belief that makes you angry, perhaps choose red. And if you're really happy with something you believe, maybe colour it yellow.

Reframe

Let's take just one of the beliefs you want to change and reframe it. For example, if you feel that people always disappoint you or let you down, try to give this some more positive language. If you wrote something like 'People always let me down', for instance, you could reframe it like this: *Although I've been hurt in the past, I know that not everybody is the same. Today I'm making myself a promise to give people a chance.*

Our beliefs are shaped by lots of things. We are influenced by people, experiences and memories, to name a few. This means that, unfortunately, some things we believe are actually false and unhelpful. We could believe, for instance, that all friends are unreliable or all partners cheat. These things are not true and won't help us to form relationships. Truth is like healthy water and food: it builds us and gives us life. Lies are like a poison, which seeps into our hearts and causes damage over time. We need to make sure our beliefs are sound. So let's take a moment to bring them to God in prayer.

God, I want to build my life on truth. Here in this moment, I bring all my ideas and beliefs before You, asking that You would help me to sort them out. Help me clear out anything untrue and unhelpful, leaving only healthy, life-giving beliefs behind. If there are deep-rooted lies I have absorbed from friends, family, TV or social media, help me to see them and hand them to You. Thank You for Your grace, which means I can take my time to consider what I truly believe in my heart. Amen.

Part 1: What you believe about God

> If you have faith as small as a mustard seed, you can say to this mulberry tree, 'Be uprooted and planted in the sea,' and it will obey you.
>
> LUKE 17:6

If you've chosen to work through this journal, I'm guessing that you have at least a small amount of faith. I've called the journal *Known* because, as Christians, we believe that we are seen, loved and known by our Creator. But before we can grasp what an incredible thing that is, we need to spend a little time putting what we believe about God into the spotlight.

Everyone reading this will be at a different place with faith. You may not be a regular church-goer or identify as a committed Christian. On the other hand, you might be a passionate, established believer. Whatever the measure of your faith, if you have even the tiniest spark within, you're in pretty good shape according to Scripture. The Bible says that faith as small as a tiny mustard seed can move mountains.

Life can shake our faith. Difficult times can cause us to doubt God's existence, nature or even if He loves us. Bad experiences with religion or other believers can leave us questioning if it's all just nonsense or a waste of time. But if you've picked up this journal, then chances are you are searching for God's voice in some way. Maybe you're hoping you'll flip open the pages and see something that makes sense to you. Perhaps you just want to feel valuable, known and loved.

Whatever the case, God knows the journey you've taken has shaped what you believe. So no matter how you feel, you can't shock Him or put Him off you. Let's just say for now that *everyone*'s faith is a work in progress and God won't turn away just because we have issues or doubts. He won't close the door because we are confused. He is always there to welcome us with open arms.

To get things started, let's plot where we are on this faith tank. Colour in or circle the temperature of your faith right now. There is no right or wrong response and absolutely no judgement. Remember, it's healthy and important to be completely honest.

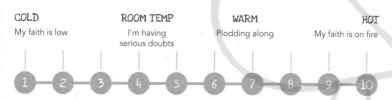

COLD	ROOM TEMP	WARM	HOT
My faith is low	I'm having serious doubts	Plodding along	My faith is on fire

1   2   3   4   5   6   7   8   9   10

Now take a couple of minutes to think about your response. Has it surprised you? Don't worry if your faith tank is a little low right now; there are bound to be reasons for that. Before we get into what Scripture says, let's unpack our beliefs about God a bit more. Using as much (or as little) creative flair as you like, write down any words that come to mind when you think about who God might be. I've included some for you to circle or shade if it helps. It doesn't matter how well you know the Bible or where you are with religion. Just be truthful and be yourself.

Loving

Hope

Goodness

Generous

Healer

Love

Holy

Absent

Mercy

Forgiving

Silent

Shame

Father

Angry

Religion

Peace

Cruel

Sin

Justice

Hope

Judgement

Joy

Provider

_____

_____

_____

_____

_____

_____

Being honest in this might have been difficult or even upsetting. You might be reflecting on the way you feel about God and perhaps it's triggering some unsettling feelings or questions. Let's take a second to deal with that in prayer.

Lord, I'm not always sure exactly what I feel or believe about You. But I want to see You as You really are. I want a true understanding of Your nature. Please help me to take any lies or misconceptions about You and deal with them. Amen.

What God says about who He is

Everyone has their own stories and thoughts about God because He can never be fully contained or explained. It's not easy to summarise what God says about Himself throughout the Bible because it is filled from beginning to end with His many names and characteristics. But just for a brief refresher, let's look at a few things that show we are *Known* and loved by a pretty incredible God.

GOD IS YOUR CREATOR

So God created mankind in his own image, in the image of God he created them; male and female he created them.

GENESIS 1:27

God, the Master of the universe, the Author of sunsets, thunderstorms, ecosystems, creatures and *everything* we love in this world also invented you. You were the original Genius's bright idea and everything about you—body, mind and soul—was invented by Him. So however you feel about yourself today, be assured you're a grand design!

GOD IS YOUR FRIEND

Greater love has no one than this: to lay down one's life for one's friends.

JOHN 15:13

As Christians, we believe that Jesus laid down His life for us as His friends. His friendship has been guaranteed from day one of *your* life. He has been present with you during every twist and turn of your journey. He has counted every tear, seen every grazed knee, every broken heart and every argument you've ever had. He has been with you through your private pain, your mistakes and in all those moments you'd rather forget. He is and always has been on your side, wanting only what is best for you.

GOD IS LOVE

God is love. Whoever lives in love lives in God, and God in them.

1 JOHN 4:16

Those who believe in God are often depicted as being judgemental, self-righteous and hateful. But the overarching theme of the Bible is **love**. It's true— many terrible things have been done in the name of God throughout history. But Scripture is crystal clear: **we are called to love one another**. John 13:35 says: *'By this everyone will know that you are my disciples, if you love one another.'* Love is the only true ID card of a believer. People who believe in God should stand out from the crowd as the ones who love each other best. So there you have it! We can no longer blame God for any hateful words or actions because Scripture is clear. Anyone who is hateful does not represent Him. Full stop.

This doesn't mean that God is all soft and fluffy. Although He is loving, forgiving, gracious and compassionate, He also means business. Just like a no-nonsense parent, God deals with things head-on. When you love your children, you want the best for them and that means boundaries. Sometimes it means encouraging them to do things they don't want to do or steering them away from things they *think* they want to do!

> because the LORD corrects the person he loves, just as a father corrects the son he delights in.
>
> PROVERBS 3:12 ISV

God's correction is the loving kind that shows us how to do things right. An example from my own world now ... My six-week-  old baby hasn't yet figured out how to go to sleep when she's tired. At first, I couldn't work out why she would cry relentlessly from 6 p.m. every night. I googled it and asked other parents who shared similar experiences. Lots of people seemed to think it was tummy pain, so we treated her for that. But I soon began to understand that, in reality, she just needed more sleep. Newborns often need help to fall asleep or they become overtired and begin to fight it. After a few nights of bundling her up and rocking her to sleep at an earlier time, the crying stopped. It wasn't what she wanted, but it was what she needed. This is what parenting is about. Sometimes God doesn't give us what we think we want because He knows what we need. And down the road, we usually see that He was right all along.

GOD IS A FAIR JUDGE

Righteousness and justice are the foundation of your throne; love and faithfulness go before you.

PSALM 89:14

If we are God's children and He loves us unconditionally, you might ask, *'Why doesn't He just let us off when we make mistakes?'* But if you really think about it, that wouldn't be good parenting. It wouldn't be justice and it wouldn't be fair. I've heard it explained like this and I think it absolutely captures the picture:

Imagine that God is like a judge in his courtroom. He is a wise and fair judge, who always sees that justice is done. That's what we want from our justice system, right? Now imagine that the judge arrives in court one day to find his own child on trial. The child has done something illegal, perhaps even something that hurt someone else, and the penalty is a heavy fine. Now, the judge loves his child and doesn't want him to suffer. But he also has a job to do. Someone has to pay the price for what has happened. In order for the judge to remain fair, he has to issue the heavy fine, even to his own kid. But after doing so, he takes off his judge's gown, steps down from the bench, goes into his chambers and writes the cheque to pay the fine himself.

When God sent His only Son Jesus to die, it was like the judge taking off his robe, stepping down from the bench and writing the cheque with his own hand. Justice was served and the judge protected his child.

There was a lot going on in that section! Not every part of this journal will contain so much dense content. But let's take the pressure off now by allowing our brains to let it all go. It's all written down if we need it again.

> Lord, thank You that You are so many wonderful things. Help me to know You better and to believe the truth about You. Help me to firmly grasp who You are to me, that I can know You in my own unique way. Amen.

Reframe

Let's take a moment now to focus on one aspect of who God says He is and ask for help to understand it. Perhaps you want to know God more as a friend. Perhaps you need help seeing God as a father. Use the space below to jot down some thoughts about it and empty your mind.

Part 2: What you believe about yourself

> For you created my inmost being; you knit me together in my mother's womb. I praise you because I am fearfully and wonderfully made;
>
> PSALM 139:13–14

Foundational beliefs

No matter what stage of life you're in, your relationship with who you are is always changing. In this section, we will look at what we believe about ourselves and how it affects our lives.

The things we learn early in life are crucial. Because children are such sponges and place so much trust in those around them, most of us have some false beliefs cemented into our foundations. There's a good chance we heard unhelpful things when we were children. We might have been called names in the playground or teased by siblings. Even great parents say potentially damaging things from time to time. Some of us have even suffered horrible abuse by others.

Our beliefs are like a house we are building, brick by brick. Everything we hear and experience lays another brick in the wall. Some bricks come from things we have overheard or shared in conversation. Some come from books or articles we've read, posts we've seen online or billboards we've passed in the street. Others come from the way we've been treated, or things we have been through.

The earlier in life we learn something, the harder it can be to unlearn. Even though we grow and change, we still often build on shaky old beliefs. When a brick is in the foundations of who we are, it isn't easy to remove. Delving into those foundations can change our whole outlook on life. It's not an easy process. But if we want to live a strong and stable life, built on truth, we have to roll our sleeves up and get to work. Sometimes we need to do a little demolition before we can rebuild.

Finding the Bad Bricks

If at an early age we get the message we're not good enough, we can spend years building our lives around that belief. We can invest all our time and attention into proving our worth to others. We'll likely go on to make poor choices based on our absence of self-worth. We might allow others to take advantage of us or treat us with a lack of respect. When this causes chaos in our lives, we continue building on top of the rubble. Bricks labelled *'I'm hopeless at relationships'* or *'There's something wrong with me'* stack up on top of the mess beneath. Until we remove the lie that we're not good enough, we will struggle to build healthy relationships.

The same is true for any lie we believe from an early age. Until we tackle those false beliefs in our foundations, we'll continue to see problems running through the walls of our lives. The good news is, it's always possible to rebuild our beliefs. And when we do, it can change the course of our lives for the better.

For the next few minutes, we're going to consider our deepest beliefs about who we are. Coming up are two groups of words. The first group describes strengths. The second describes what we might identify as weaknesses. Circle **every word** you **believe** applies to you. You can add your own words too as they come to mind. Don't forget, there is no one reading or grading your answers. This is just for you.

Don't take more than five minutes over this. Remember, we are looking to find out what we believe and the truth often comes to mind first.

Strengths

I am:

Friendly   Loving   Forgiving   Attractive

Punctual   Organised   Thoughtful

Honest   Kind   Generous   Fun

Intelligent   Talented   Positive

Beautiful   Loyal   Consistent   Helpful

Trustworthy   Creative   Hardworking   Tidy

Confident   Clean   Wise

Weaknesses
I am:

Disorganised   Shy   Unattractive   Dishonest

Average   Always late   Cautious

Lazy   Messy   Forgetful   Negative

Insecure   Jealous   Anxious   Chaotic

Easily angered   Boring   Unwell

Depressive   Unpopular   Aggressive   Fearful

Cowardly   Clumsy   Inconsistent

....

....

Reflect and Reframe

Reflect

How does it look? Take a moment to count how many words you circled in each group and include any you added. Which group did you find yourself mostly circling? Do you find it easier to list your strengths or your weaknesses? What does this tell you about the way you see yourself? If you found it easier to list weaknesses, perhaps there are some beliefs in your foundations that need to be removed. What were your reasons for seeing these particular weaknesses? Has someone spoken this over you at an early age? Write some notes below.

With every major life change, our self-belief gets a shake-up. I'll never forget the way my confidence was challenged when I started

Story Time

secondary school. By my final year of primary, I'd become content and secure. I had some of the best grades in the class and a great group of friends I'd known since day one. I felt I knew who I was: a well-liked, clever kid, who was generally happy. But that all came crashing down when I started secondary school.

I was so excited on the first day of Year 7, with my crisp new uniform and freshly sharpened pencils. *Finally,* I thought, *I can be a little more grown up. I'll make tons of new friends and get to study my favourite subjects.* But as early as day three, I was feeling quite lost. It became clear that I needed to be far more responsible and organised, and it seemed I wasn't a natural at either. I had next to no sense of direction, which had never been an issue in my tiny primary school. But in the vast, busy corridors of secondary, it was overwhelming. I was often last to make it to lessons, leaving few seats to choose from. I would usually end up sitting alone and, as a result, struggled to make friends.

On top of that, the new subjects were a stretch for me. It became apparent that I'd been very much in my comfort zone at primary school, in a world where creative writing and arts were things I could easily focus on. When it came to the sciences, I was bottom of the class. I got so used to being confused that I stopped putting up my hand to ask for help. I lost all the confidence I'd once had in my abilities. I stopped believing I was a likeable, clever kid and began to believe I was average and unattractive. I quickly became quite depressed and made every excuse to miss school.

What followed was four years of mostly misery. Things only got better in Year 11 when I finally made friends and took subject options I could excel at. But my low self-esteem had affected my mental health so badly, I'd missed up to a third of my schooling. It was too late to catch up on some of the important stuff and I got pretty terrible results in most subjects.

This wasn't easy to come to terms with, knowing how much promise I'd shown at primary level. I was desperate to rediscover the confidence I'd had in Year 6, before I got lost in a sea of self-doubt. I began to carry around some negative beliefs about myself. I believed I was a failure. I believed I was incapable of achieving my goals. I'd forgotten that I was creative, gifted and loveable.

The great news is that God did an incredible work of restoration in my life (more on that later). With His help I was able to work on some deconstruction of those negative foundational beliefs. By focusing on what Scripture had to say, I could begin to slowly rebuild my life on truth.

In spite of not having the greatest time at school, I've been able to achieve lots of my goals in life. I've toured the world as a musician and even become a published author! This was only possible because God took me down to the bare bricks of my beliefs and did some demolition.

Today, we are going to start building a new wall of beliefs about ourselves based on what God says. Here are **five amazing Scriptures** to get you  started. Once you've read them, why not decide what feels most relevant to you and put some key words into the wall on page 55.

> You are altogether beautiful,
> my love; there is no flaw in you.
>
> SONG OF SONGS 4:7 ESV

This Scripture is from an amazing book in the Bible all about love. It is pretty much the manual for romance and perfectly describes the state of being besotted by someone. The whole book has a dual meaning. As well as being a commentary on love between people, it also represents God's love for

His people, including YOU. That means you are *'altogether beautiful'*. Never forget it! Build it into your foundations today.

> For we are God's handiwork, created in Christ Jesus to do good works, which God prepared in advance for us to do.
>
> EPHESIANS 2:10

We will come back to this in the 'Purpose' section. For now, just focus on the *'God's handiwork'* part. You were hand-crafted by the Master of the universe. The same force who formed mountains, stars, oceans, rainbows, creatures and all things beautiful also crafted you! Build the belief that you are *'God's handiwork'* into your foundations today.

> But you are a chosen people, a royal priesthood, a holy nation
>
> 1 PETER 2:9

You are personally chosen by God. That's pretty good news. He hand-selected you for the team! Not only that but after He chose you, He crowned you and gave you a royal title. There is no greater honour in earthly terms than to be chosen by the King and called royalty! Put *'royalty'* into your foundations now.

> This means that anyone who belongs to Christ has become a new person. The old life is gone; a new life has begun!
>
> 2 CORINTHIANS 5:17 NLT

People love new things. There's nothing quite like unboxing a new gadget, putting on a pristine pair of trainers or breaking the spine of a new book. New is awesome. But very often we don't *feel* quite so shiny. Life can leave us a bit dusty and worn out. We know we've made mistakes and we're a little scratched and bruised by what we've been through. God takes our old self and exchanges it for something completely untarnished. Why not build the words *'new creation'* into your foundations today.

> The Spirit himself testifies with our spirit that we are God's children. Now if we are children, then we are heirs – heirs of God and co-heirs with Christ
>
> ROMANS 8:16–17

When I was younger, I had a lot of envy for people like Paris Hilton, heiress to the Hilton Hotel chain and business empire. Before she'd done any work or achieved anything, she was already set up for life. But the good news, in spiritual terms, is we are too. When we become a part of God's family, our inheritance is His kingdom. Why not build 'heir to the kingdom' into your foundational beliefs right now.

Time to Pray

It's not easy to take apart and rebuild ourselves. It's not easy to change the beliefs of a lifetime. Let's take a moment to give the foundations of our lives to God.

Lord, I give You this new wall of beliefs. I ask that You would help me remove any brick that builds an unhealthy belief. If there are any lies built deeply into me, please remove them right now, in Jesus' name. Help me to build my self-image on truth and on Your Word. Amen.

A new commandment I give to you,
that you love one another:

JOHN 13:34 ESV

The way we view others drastically affects our lives. As well as having a direct impact on our relationships, it is often a reflection of how we feel about ourselves too. Often our judgements of others and their lives are like holding up a mirror to our own hearts and minds. In this section, we're going to examine our hearts and ask God to help us gain a healthier perspective on the people in our world.

The filtered view and the rear view

When it comes to the way we view others, there are two common traps we fall into. We'll call these 'the filtered view' and 'the rear view'.

'The filtered view' is the view clouded by our own ideas. Often, the ideas we have about other people are unrealistic. Even though we *know* nobody is perfect, always happy or always gets it right, we still tend to presume others are doing better in life than we are. A lot of this has to do with social media (which we'll look at a little later in the journal).

'The rear view' is the view clouded by our past. Our experiences have a lot to answer for. We often carry our past hurts into our present relationships. We walk into new friendships with old offences still imprinted on our minds. If we've been deceived or abused, it can lead to a mistrust of people who've done nothing wrong by us. Even though we know everyone is different, we struggle to let go of the ideas we've built in our minds.

Whether it's trust issues or false ideas, beliefs about others can shape both our present and our future. We can easily sabotage a perfectly good thing by struggling to let go of the past. And we can find ourselves avoiding opportunities if we fear others will judge us, take advantage or let us down. But we want to be people who are free from the past. Although our experiences have helped to shape who we are, we don't want them to define us. Here are a couple of stories to help us meditate on these thoughts.

Helen was in her twenties when she went into business with her best friend Diane. They both invested all their savings as well as hours of  their time into getting it going, growing it from the ground up. Eventually, their hard work paid off and they managed to open a boutique on the high street. Helen, feeling secure in the relationship, didn't mind using her own name to secure the rental contract on the shop. But she was hugely disappointed by what followed. Diane got into a new relationship and started to come into work less and less. It was obvious she was losing interest in the project. Helen continued to give her friend the benefit of the doubt, not wanting to believe that things were falling apart. Then, out of the blue, Diane announced she was leaving the business to begin a new venture. Despite every effort to change her friend's mind, Helen was left with all the bills and no business partner. Helen was shocked and devastated by this betrayal of her trust and their friendship ended as a result. The betrayal was deep and affected her for years. She had such trust issues, she struggled to form good friendships and, after winding down the business, decided not to do anything similar again.

Katie had grown up in a very turbulent home environment. When she was eight years old, after years of constant fighting, her parents finally divorced. Some years later, Katie found out that one of them had been unfaithful, which had ultimately led to the breakdown of the marriage. When Katie started dating in her late teens she just couldn't seem to 'pick the right guy'. And even when things were going well, she struggled to trust the person she was in a relationship with. She would often go through her boyfriend's phone or read his emails, worried he might be hiding something. Katie never connected the dots, but because of what had happened in her parents' marriage, she had a deep-rooted belief that people couldn't be trusted and would eventually let her down. It was ruining her ability to connect with others and ultimately making her unhappy.

In both these stories, the rear view was impacting lives negatively. Both girls needed to do some healing, letting go and forgiving. Not because the people who'd hurt them deserved it, but because these girls deserved to live a life of freedom.

Take a five-minute break now and go to a safe, quiet space. Close your eyes if you need to, breathe deeply and try to empty your mind. Now ask yourself: *'Do I have trust issues? Is there someone I need to forgive so that I can have a clean slate for future relationships? Or have I been looking at others through a filter, believing they are more "together" than I am?'* Meditate on these questions and, if anything comes to mind, write it down.

....

....

....

....

....

....

When it comes to others, God's perspective is super clear in Scripture: our job is to love them. Admittedly this can be a challenge. Sometimes people

do such hurtful or antisocial things it makes loving them almost impossible. But even when it's hard for us, God says we should always try to **love the person in front of us**. That means loving people in spite of:

- our past hurts
- our insecurities
- our impressions
- their behaviour

If we mistrust others because of someone else's mistakes, that's not love. **Love is a clean slate.** Love **trusts** and looks for the **truth**. Love should be the filter through which we pass every thought, word and action.

Take a look at this amazing passage of Scripture. Does any of it stand out to you? Why not shade in some of the key words. If you struggle with envy, could you colour the word in and ask God to help you with that?

> Love is *patient*, love is kind. It does not *envy*, it does not boast, it is not *proud*. It does not dishonour others, it is not self-seeking, it is not easily *angered*, it keeps no *record of wrongs*. Love does not delight in evil but rejoices with the truth. It always protects, always *trusts*, always hopes, always *perseveres*. Love never fails.
>
> 1 CORINTHIANS 13:4–8 (EMPHASIS MINE)

Time to Pray

If you've been hurt in the past, you probably deserved better. You may have every right to feel hurt and angry. But you need to be a person who is free from the past. You need freedom to go after opportunities without fear of being betrayed or let down. You need freedom to experience loving relationships. If anything from this part of the journal has struck a chord with you, invite God into that through prayer.

Lord, I need Your help to be free from the past. I don't want my experiences to cloud my view or to live with false ideas of other people. Even when it's hard, please help me to live out this Scripture about love. Help me to approach my relationships according to Your amazing Word. If I'm struggling to forgive someone who has hurt me or let me down, help me to work on that and make progress. And, God, when I see others living what looks like the perfect life, help me let go of my false ideas and see people who need love. Amen.

Section Three

Who we are online

The internet is a bit like a new planet we're exploring. It's exotic, exciting and filled with possibility, but there are also dangers and poisons we don't yet understand. There are toxins we don't yet have names for. We need to explore with caution.

Anything is possible online. The web has made billionaires out of tech students, and household names out of dreamers, singing, dancing and putting on make-up in their bedrooms! It also gives us instant access to the people we love and admire most. We can '@' our favourite celebs or companies and get immediate responses. We never need lose touch with family or friends again! We might even find the love of our lives online.

But the web is not always a positive space. Like most revolutionary inventions, the internet has its pros and cons. Whole lives have been left in tatters as a result of a single, poorly worded tweet that went viral. People have faced devastating consequences as their intimate texts and pictures have been shared without their consent. So-called 'revenge porn' has ruined lives. That's all before we even consider cyberbullying and its potentially disastrous repercussions.

Part 1: Put your truth filter on

In so many ways, the internet is like a superpower we haven't yet mastered. But let's be honest, it isn't going anywhere. Lots of us use platforms like TikTok, Facebook and Instagram on a daily basis. So, while we are out there, we need to armour up. If we're going to be social media users with a strong sense of identity, we need to get ready to put a new type of filter on: the **filter of God's truth**.

The internet is taking its toll on our self-image. The demand for cosmetic surgeries and procedures has surged since the launch of platforms like Instagram and Snapchat, with a staggering number of people wanting to look more like their selfies. It's no coincidence that mental health in young people has rapidly declined alongside the rise of social media. According to the latest stats (correct at time of publishing), there are now around **4.20 billion** users around the world, equivalent to more than **53 per cent** of the global population. A lot of us spend more than two hours each day, scrolling, liking, commenting and posting. Mental health charities and organisations have observed a connection between the time we spend online and the way we feel about ourselves.

It's definitely not all bad. During periods of isolation, social media has provided a way to connect, share encouragement and rally for great causes. As a recording artist and someone who works in ministry, I've always tried to use the platforms for good. But alongside the positives, we need to be mindful of what they can do to our sense of identity. We're going to explore that now ...

 How is social media making you feel? Have you noticed it having a negative effect on you? Do you feel you depend on it for distraction/ entertainment? We're going to do an experiment now. If you're an Instagram or Facebook user, **open your app and time five minutes**. For those five minutes, observe your thoughts. Try to hear in your head what the images are making you think and feel, and jot down your thoughts below. I'll share mine after yours ...

MY UNFILTERED SCROLLING THOUGHTS ...

- *I haven't worked out in ages; I should shape up.*

- *I must order some of those for my baby.*

- *It's so lovely to see my friend's little boy growing up.*

- *I wish I was on that trip.*

- *I can't wait to get some sunshine.*

- *I wish I had the same opportunities as that particular recording artist.*

- *I'm missing out on so much career development right now.*

These were my actual unfiltered thoughts during scrolling. As you can see, there were a couple of positives! But if I observe what I'm feeling, this is what I notice: first, I'm fighting the thought that I might be failing in some way. I feel I could be doing more for my career and should be working harder. Secondly, I feel I could look a lot better if I really tried. Overall, not great! What I notice more than anything is a desire to be more like the people on my feed; whether it's their toned abs or their incredible careers.

Born to transform

We are born with the instinct to see, learn and grow. My baby girl is changing incredibly fast at the moment.

Almost every time she wakes, she displays a new skill or facial expression. Each day, she watches me closely, storing up everything she sees in her fresh little hard drive of a brain. It's as though she is constantly downloading information from her environment and quickly adding it to her library of behaviours. She does this because that is what her amazing biology has programmed her to do.

We too are watching, learning and becoming what we see each day. When we focus on other people it naturally follows that we begin to imitate them. Some of the most popular images on Instagram are those that show body transformations via fitness and diet regimes. Spend too long scrolling those and you're almost certain to start comparing your body to those in the pictures. Fitness and health are important, of course. But like anything, when we focus too hard on these things it becomes unhealthy and can be damaging to both our minds and bodies.

where the Spirit of the Lord
is, there is freedom. And we
all, who with unveiled faces
contemplate the Lord's glory,
are being transformed into his image with
ever-increasing glory

2 CORINTHIANS 3:17–18

This Scripture is pretty incredible when you put it into the context of social media. First it says, *'where the Spirit of the Lord is, there is freedom.'* Okay. So do we feel *'free'* when we spend hours scrolling? Or do we feel we're being dragged into the same negative thoughts over and over? Take a look at what you wrote in the Honesty First section. Are those thoughts helping you to improve your life or are they more likely to make you dissatisfied?

If the thoughts you have while scrolling leave you feeling inadequate or anxious, it might be time to rethink how much headspace you're giving your online life. This Scripture in Corinthians reminds us that what **we focus on has the power to change us**. The stuff we give our attention to can bring us freedom or it can enslave us.

The verses go on to say: *'we all, who with unveiled faces contemplate the **Lord's** glory, are being transformed into **his** image with ever-increasing glory'* (emphasis mine). This basically explains that what we *'contemplate'* has a transforming effect on who we are, for better or worse. Hours spent scrolling can cause us to focus on the beauty, achievements and popularity of other people. Essentially, we end up contemplating the 'glory' of our friends and even of strangers. This clearly doesn't help us to be free. In fact, it leaves us chasing an illusion, enslaved to an idea of who we should be.

Corinthians reminds us that focusing on God's glory helps us to transform into *His* likeness. Focusing on God's character and beauty will help us to become like Him, which will lead us into a life that is full, rather than a life that is full of self-doubt.

Have you been focusing too much on the way other people look, act and live their lives? Has it been making you feel insecure or uneasy about where you are in life? It's not always easy to move our focus away from others and onto God, so let's ask for His help.

Lord, I know that social media isn't going anywhere. If I must use it, help me to put on the filter of Your truth. Remind me not to focus so hard on others that I lose sight of what really matters in my life. Help me not to compare myself with the people I admire, because ultimately You haven't called me to become like someone else. You've called me to be the very best version of myself and to be more like You. In Jesus' name. Amen.

Part 2: Tweaking those pics

What we see online is not a reflection of reality. Even though we already know this, it's important to remind ourselves. We've all seen the 'Instagram versus reality' memes. They can teach us a lot. Everything attractive and exciting on Instagram has been styled well, lit well and framed well, often featuring models or influencers who fit a certain stereotype of beauty. This process has set a tricky standard for what gets the most engagement. Just a few moments browsing will show you that glossy, flawless-looking pictures draw the most attention. Whether we notice it or not, we will probably find ourselves trying to achieve the same results.

Software for editing selfies is just a click away in the app store. We can create a whole new version of ourselves in seconds; a version that better resembles the stereotypes we've become used to seeing. So … is this a problem? It's just a little creativity and fun, right? To some degree, yes. It's fun to see what we might look like with a tinier waist, broader hips or a peachier rump. It's pretty cool to be able to apply a more 'snatched' make-up look with just a thumb swipe. But spending a lot of time on things like this, or feeling you *have* to do it, could be affecting your mental health and your sense of identity.

Four ways your 'pic-tweaking' could be causing you harm

IT'S CHANGING THE WAY YOU SEE YOURSELF

Loving who you are begins with embracing the real you. Filtering and editing your pictures can slowly begin to warp your self-image. If you get used to seeing your edited self in pictures, there's a good chance you'll start to find your real reflection harder to accept. Keeping your online appearance more real will help you have deeper security in who God made you to be. Plus, every time someone hits 'like' on a picture that actually looks like you, it will boost your confidence!

IT'S CAUSING YOU TO OBSESS ABOUT 'FLAWS'

Most of us have minor face and body hang-ups. Ever heard a friend say something like, 'My eyes are too far apart' or 'My ears aren't symmetrical' and wondered what the heck they were talking about? Time spent close up to the mirror or zooming in on selfies makes us more likely to obsess about small things. We can become acutely insecure about things that other people don't even notice! Reshaping things with an app can give us an exaggerated perception of something completely normal. We might even end up wanting to change those things for real.

IT ADDS TO A WIDER PROBLEM

You might be tweaking your pics because social media puts you under pressure to 'measure up'. But every time you succumb to that pressure by changing your body or face with an app, you're becoming a part of the problem. We want our pictures to be pleasing to look at but we don't want to make others feel down about themselves and under pressure to be more like us. Every time you post something real, you are encouraging others to be themselves too.

IT COULD BE AFFECTING YOUR WELL-BEING IN OTHER WAYS

Integrity is important for mental health. Presenting ourselves in a false way can make us feel a bit like frauds. We might start to suffer with something called 'imposter syndrome' (the feeling that you're not really who people think or expect you to be). If we get comfortable under a blanket of filters, we may become less confident about people seeing us in the flesh.

Do not conform to the pattern of this world, but be transformed by the renewing of your mind.

ROMANS 12:2

If we really want to 'transform', we need to make over the way we think, not the way we look. The pattern of this world, especially online, is to conform to the latest trends. If large backsides are 'in' we work out like crazy or tweak our pics till we match up. But our bodies and faces are not problems that need to be fixed. Your natural shape shouldn't feel like an inconvenience, standing in the way of your success. **The problem is the way we see ourselves, not the way we look.** God has already told us we are His workmanship and that He knows every detail of our bodies and faces. He has placed a beauty within us that is entirely unique. Trends come and go; God made you to last a lifetime.

Unless you live in the middle of nowhere, trends in fashion, entertainment and pop culture are hard to ignore. If we're going to see ourselves through God's eyes, we need His help—daily. We need to regularly ask God to give us revelation of our value and unique beauty. If we can be transformed by the renewing of our minds, we might even begin to love the things about ourselves we used to dislike. Let's give it a try …

Lord, when You created me, You had more than social media in mind. It's not always easy to ignore what's popular online. But within me You designed a beauty that is unique and timeless. Help me to see and embrace it. I want to be real. I want to help create a culture that sets others free. Please guide me, by the Holy Spirit, to see my own beauty and be confident in sharing it with others. Amen.

Take a moment to study your face in the mirror. Is there something about it you've ever wished was more 'Instagram worthy'? The current trends include things like lip-filler for fuller lips, heavily contoured cheeks and nose for the 'snatched' look. But these things are exactly that—trends! What if you were to create your own trend: the trend of loving and embracing what you already have? Let's take something we've been tempted to change in the past and reframe the way we think about it. Write down one thing you've considered changing about your look and instead decide that it's already perfect. You might write something like: *My body shape is bang on trend! In the past I've wanted to tweak and change it. But as of this moment, I'm deciding that it's perfect.*

Part 3: Social media 'FOMO' (Fear Of Missing Out)

Social media adds to our insecurity on many levels. As well as causing us to compare ourselves physically, it often causes us to compare:

- our social lives
- our relationships
- our homes and 'stuff'
- our talents
- our popularity
- our professional lives and opportunities

These kinds of comparisons can deeply affect our sense of identity and even our mental health. When we're casually scrolling and see something that triggers us, it can be powerful enough to ruin an entire day, chipping away at our confidence and filling our minds with doubt. In this section, we will look at some super **positive thoughts and affirmations**, so that we're armed to deal with those triggers when they come. Next time you feel upset by comparison, come back to this and meditate on some good thoughts!

The trigger: comparing our social lives

We've all been there. You sit down to enjoy a night in: snacks, Netflix and maybe a pet at your side. You even have a cute new cactus on your dresser that looks beautifully 'Pinterest worthy'. It's all very nice. So, you open your favourite app ready to post a selfie. But, whoa—the bubble quickly bursts when you see several of your friends together, dressed to the nines and checking in somewhere exciting. You suddenly feel drab with your messy bun and flannel shirt. After the initial sting of realising you're not there, the questions begin … *Why wasn't I invited? What's wrong with me? Why is my life so boring?* And it goes on. Suddenly the boxset and cat lose their appeal. You start to question yourself and even your worth.

The cure

When you see posts of exciting social occasions, remember, they are just that—'occasions'. The people in those pictures aren't doing something exciting all the time (even if it seems that way). They have plenty of solo, box-set nights too and feel exactly the same when they open their socials. In fact, they're probably excited to be out and about and that's why they took a picture and posted it for you to see! Next time you're out, you probably will too. It's important to remember: **other people's**

pictures aren't about you. Just because *they* were invited doesn't mean *you* deliberately weren't. Just because they're beautiful doesn't mean you're not.

The trigger: comparing our relationships

It peaks during any national holiday and especially around Valentine's. But anytime pictures of couples and families surge can leave us feeling insecure and even lonely. Couples by the Christmas tree or sipping drinks on a beach, kids in matching PJs, all smiles and candy canes, can make us feel inadequate. Even when we're in a romantic relationship or have great family lives, the looks of joy on Instagram faces can leave us wondering if our relationships are the only ones that need work.

The cure

Don't read too much into people's family portraits. The truth is, no relationship or family is perfect. Every family has issues and every couple has arguments. There's no way to tell what's really going on behind the smiles. And even when a relationship is good, life is not without its trials. No one, from the richest to the poorest, single, married, with or without kids, has an easy life. We all encounter loss, sickness, grief and personal struggle. Try to remember that the picture is exactly that: just a picture.

The trigger: comparing our home or 'stuff'

This is a big one for lots of us. Instagram is one big brag-fest, from luxury homes to designer handbags. Whether it's an influencer or your classmate, someone will always seem to have the latest look, gadget or desirable item.

The cure

Remember that stuff is just 'stuff'. No one, however rich or privileged, can take their stuff with them beyond this life. It doesn't equal happiness or contentment. It isn't a sign of a full life. Plenty of people have everything they want materially but aren't satisfied. If you work hard enough you can acquire many material things. But the best things in life aren't 'things' at all. God's love, forgiveness and favour can't be earnt. They are gifts that belong to us by grace. As a result, God calls us to store up our treasures in heaven not on earth, where they're bound to rust and disappear.

The trigger: comparing our talents

There are a lot of talented people online. YouTube has shown us the levels of genius in our midst. It doesn't take long to find someone who is more able than we are (and probably younger). It can be enough to make you consider giving up on your dreams.

The cure

Remember that no one can be you. Talent might be impressive but being a blessing is a whole other level. When you find the courage to be completely yourself, sharing your unique experiences and gifts, no one can outshine you. If you see other people in their element, don't try to be like them. Realise they got there by being themselves.

The trigger: comparing our popularity

Social media has turned us all into content creators and influencers! But instead of empowering us, this often makes us feel invisible. Ever posted a picture that didn't get much interaction and wanted to take it down immediately? I know I have. It's hard not to look at the accounts that get a ton of likes, shares and follows and not feel disastrously unpopular.

The cure

Realise first that popularity doesn't always equate to value. What would you say is more useful in God's eyes—an account that reaches 200 million people with an airbrushed bikini shot or an account that shares encouragement and truth with 200 people? That's an easy one. Well, then, what about an account that shares truth with 200 million people?

That would be great! And with a little work you might get there. But if you don't, don't sweat it. It's not your job to be anyone but you. So long as you're doing what you feel you should do, and doing it well, that's all that matters.

The trigger: comparing our professional lives and opportunities

This can be tough if you're working hard to achieve your dreams. You might see that someone else landed a job with a company that rejected your application. You might feel the same people get picked for things time and again and it's never you. Or you might feel you are progressing at a much slower pace than your peers.

The cure

Yes, it can sting. But this is where faith must kick in. God has a plan for you. That plan is like no other. It's a mistake to look at anyone else's success and put it beside your own journey. Can you work harder? Perhaps. Perhaps there are steps you can take to help move things along. But ultimately, if you're putting things in God's hands and asking for His help every day, you can trust that you're at the centre of His will.

Here are four Scriptures to pull you out of your social media insecurity and 'FOMO':

BE THANKFUL

Rejoice always, pray continually, give thanks in all circumstances; for this is God's will for you in Christ Jesus.

1 THESSALONIANS 5:16–18

BE FAITHFUL

'For I know the plans I have for you,' declares the LORD, 'plans to prosper you and not to harm you, plans to give you hope and a future.'

JEREMIAH 29:11

BE KIND

Be kind to one another, tenderhearted, forgiving one another, as God in Christ forgave you.

EPHESIANS 4:32 ESV

BE KINGDOM-FOCUSED

Do not store up for yourselves treasures on earth, where moths and vermin destroy, and where thieves break in and steal. But store up for yourselves treasures in heaven, where moths and vermin do not destroy, and where thieves do not break in and steal. For where your treasure is, there your heart will be also.

MATTHEW 6:19–21

Gratitude is possibly the most helpful way to manage 'FOMO' and comparison triggered by social media. Instead of focusing on what other people have, bring back your focus to the good things in your own life. Take a moment to look around you and be grateful for where you are and what you're doing right now. To let someone else's fun spoil yours is a big fat waste of life.

Part 4: A lasting impression

We can't ignore that the internet is a space where most of us now exist. We do our banking, buying, dating, gaming, socialising, networking and business there. So today, **who we are online is pretty important**. The web is not just used for our entertainment. The things we view, post and share, or our 'digital footprint', can be many things including:

- a record of our words and behaviours

- a reminder of our past actions

- an archive of our past relationships

- a digital record of our browsing, clicking and buying habits

- a profile of our beliefs and interests.

It can be used by future employers and potential partners to check us out (whether we like it or not). Ex-partners and former friends can keep track of us. And businesses, charities and organisations can target us as potential customers, clients and users.

So **we need to be intentional about who we are online** because there's a good chance some of what we share will follow us. We need to realise that, while it's a creative and fun place, it's also a place where some pretty life-changing stuff can go down. It's not easy to 'un-share' things. And it's not as easy as we'd like to cover our tracks or keep things private.

Before you share/post

Ultimately, we want the way we appear online to reflect our best selves. We want it to show us in an authentic yet flattering light. Bearing in mind that future employers, friends and partners could see things, we want to leave a footprint we're proud of and won't cause us grief later. Here are some golden, helpful pointers to make sure your online profile reflects the best parts of you.

CHECK YOURSELF

It's always good to do a little self-check before sharing thoughts and opinions. Bernard Meltzer said this about speaking in general, and it goes for our online selves too:

> Before you speak, ask yourself if what you are going to say is true, is kind, is necessary, is helpful. If the answer is no, maybe what you are about to say should be left unsaid.[3]

CHECK YOUR FACTS

We want to be bringers of the truth, not unwitting spreaders of misinformation! So checking our facts is *really* important. We are often pretty reactive with what we post. If we see something that pushes our buttons, perhaps an emotional fundraiser or a post about social injustice, we feel the need to spread the word. But if we're not careful, we could be helping a lie make its way across the web at lightning speed. As the saying attributed to many different people goes,

> *A lie can travel around the world and back again while the truth is lacing up its boots.*

CONSIDER THE CONSEQUENCES

We have to remember the effect that 'likes and shares' can have on the lives of others. The internet can dismantle a career or reputation at breakneck pace. If a celeb or influencer makes a mistake, we can easily get swept up in the riptide of gossip. The safe distance we have as users browsing our feeds makes it all too easy to engage in negativity. It only takes a few moments to pass comment from behind a screen. But if the other person was in front of us, whether a celebrity, a politician or someone we know personally, would we say those things?

CONSIDER THE FUTURE

We can't possibly know where life will take us or get preoccupied trying to predict the future. But it's always worth asking, *'Will I be happy to look back on this content in five years' time?'* Intense as it sounds, it's even worth considering, *'Would I want my kids to read/see this?'* When all is said and done, it's not about being perfect. Nobody is. But we wouldn't want people to see things written a long time ago and judge our hearts by them today. Lots of people have had their careers ruined by tweets they posted years ago that no longer reflect their hearts.

TRUST NO ONE

Yes, this sounds severe. But the problem with the internet is we can never be sure who we're talking to. Fake accounts pop up using pictures of people we know in order to gain access to our info and followers. Hackers even post directly to our friends' feeds and make it sound as though we're speaking to them. A golden rule? **Don't share any intimate information online.** The same goes for pictures. A good policy is to ask, *'Would I want my nan to see this?'* If the answer is no … step away from the 'share' button! You can never be sure where a picture shared via the internet will end up. So if it's private, keep it private!

My dear brothers and sisters, take note of this: everyone should be quick to listen, slow to speak and slow to become angry

JAMES 1:19

In other words, **slow down!** We work fast when we're interacting online. In a world of filters, it's very easy to share thoughts without a verbal one. If we want to have control over how we appear online, we should take a breath before we type. Emotions can run high, especially when it comes to hot topics. Conversations or posts relating to politics or religion can spiral out of control pretty quickly. I've seen friends become enemies over a single, casual meme share. It takes less than a second to click 'share' and it can begin the undoing of a lifelong friendship. It shouldn't, but it really can.

Do not let any unwholesome talk come out of your mouths, but only what is helpful for building others up according to their needs, that it may benefit those who listen.

EPHESIANS 4:29

Lots of issues, hugely sensitive and personal in nature, have been politicised. We see a bunch of views on the daily feeds that clash with our faith and ethics. Should we be vocal about our beliefs? Sure! But the 'how' of doing that is very important. Love, again, is the key and keeping an open, respectful dialogue is essential. We are building the kingdom, not bulldozing the world!

Lord, help me have wisdom when it comes to my life online. Help me to consider how my words and actions affect others and could affect me. Help me to represent myself in a way I will still enjoy in years to come and that will reflect my best self. Help me to speak wisely and kindly. In Jesus' name. Amen.

How do you want to be perceived online? When you look back, what do you want to see and what would you want the people who love you to find?

Write some notes here to help you remember who you want to be on the web.

....

....

We should never be afraid to challenge the norm if it could be better. And when it comes to what we say and do on public platforms, we need to be held accountable. But again, when we stand up for what we believe in, it's important we act in a way that represents our best selves.

When it comes to issues like social justice, equality and climate change, young people know how to use their voices, which is an awesome thing! It's important to speak up for the oppressed and call out bad behaviour. But what begins as speaking out can quickly become a sort of public stoning when it comes to social media. When several join in agreement, a 'mob mentality' can emerge. Amid the passionate voices calling for change, some choose to simply shout, accuse and condemn. In going after anyone mercilessly, without grace or compassion, we do ourselves and God a disservice. Even in our campaigning we need to represent God's heart.

> So in everything, do to others what you would have them do to you
>
> MATTHEW 7:12

People often say things they don't mean or fully understand. I'm sure most of us have been careless with our words at one time or another. And, yes, we should be challenged when we're out of line. But it's so important to remember that everyone makes mistakes. Everyone needs space to learn, grow and evolve. 'Cancelling' someone online, even if they're horrifically wrong, doesn't allow that grace.

When someone says something on social media that we disagree with, we have a right to disagree. But we also have a responsibility to handle it the right way, especially as believers. **Love is truthful but love is also kind.** Sometimes we get so caught up in the first part that we forget the second! It's great when we're prepared to stand up for our communities and our rights. But we also need to allow people the chance to change.

If ever you see an angry mob coming for someone online because they said or did something disagreeable, pause for a moment before you become another voice in the mob. **Always put yourself in the place of the person on trial.** How would you feel in their shoes? Maybe you're thinking, *I'll never put myself in that position.* But it's actually easier to end up at the centre of a controversy than you might think. You could misjudge who will see your post or make a joke people misread. You could be falsely accused or even a victim of mistaken identity! Something you said so long ago you barely remember it, could surface unexpectedly. Private conversations can be leaked and taken out of context. Whatever the case, try to consider how it might feel to be in the firing line. Then aim to do whatever you hope others would do for you.

> If your brother or sister sins, go and point out their fault, just between the two of you.
>
> MATTHEW 18:15

Jesus says we shouldn't take up our personal issues with people publicly. For one thing, it pulls in all kinds of other opinions and voices, escalating the problem. It can also have a negative effect on people silently observing. Instead of drawing them to our cause, it can put them off altogether. So, if someone has hurt you or has a belief you disagree with, it's worth speaking with them personally. It's much better to use your public platform for drawing positive attention to the things you care about.

'Reasonable people may disagree'

This is a political quote that is absolutely true. Not everybody who disagrees with us is wrong. Being reasonable means staying open to the possibility that we might have something to learn. And let's not forget, someone can be totally wrong about something and still be a good person! Whatever the situation, we have to make room for opposing views in our lives. We can always learn from someone we disagree with, even if all we learn is that their opinion exists.

A few weeks ago, I shared something online that drew a fair bit of attention. Something had happened in the news and I was looking to bring a little balance to an argument about it. Lots of people agreed with my point of view but a few didn't. One girl left an 'angry face' emoji and went on to say how upset she was with what I'd said. Obviously I hadn't intended to upset anyone but my post had touched a nerve. She wrote a long but respectful paragraph about why she disagreed. I responded, explaining in a little more detail what I had meant. In the end, we came to an understanding and realised that our hearts were in a similar place, even though we disagreed. We thanked one another for the space to disagree peacefully and learn from each other.

If ever it is you ...

neither height nor depth, nor anything else in all creation, will be able to separate us from the love of God that is in Christ Jesus our Lord.

ROMANS 8:39

If you've ever been in the firing line, you'll know just how painful it is. You might have been challenged by someone about your lifestyle or your beliefs. You might have been the victim of bullying by strangers or peers. If anyone has ever attacked you online, it's important to know that **no one on earth has the authority to 'cancel' you**. The enemy loves to speak condemnation over what isn't his to condemn. But the enemy doesn't have the power to declare you or your story over. Next time someone tries to cancel you, remember that nothing can separate you from God's love. The mob can make all the noise they like, but God has the final say.

If you've struggled with confrontation online, been harassed or ganged-up on by others, now is the time to bring that hurt before God and ask for His healing. Maybe you've just felt forgotten, overlooked or insignificant in comparison to your peers. Bring that too …

Lord, help me to be a light to the people in my world and beyond. Even though comments and statuses are just words on a screen, I know they can affect lives in a huge way. Help me to have wisdom and to know that nothing can ever separate me from Your love. No one has the power to say my story is over. Amen.

Section Four

Core values

Your **core values** are the top things you value in your approach to living. If you were a stick of seaside rock they would be written right through you! They're already a part of who you are and they will affect who you become. Determining your core values will help you decide what you want to do with your time, how you want to do it and who you want to do it with. In other words, your values determine how you live your life.

Why should I figure out my core values?

Companies often have core values listed on a staffroom wall or in a handbook they give to staff. Your role within a company is ultimately to achieve that company's goals. For example, if you worked for a supermarket and one of their core values was 'family orientated', your job would be to carry that value with you into the office, onto the shop floor and to represent it as you work. You are not a supermarket but you are, in many ways, a brand. What matters to you is every bit as important as what matters to your boss or any other corporation you serve. You want the people in your life to know what you're about. Realising and naming what matters to you will help you prioritise those things and be a good example to others.

Part 1: What are my values?

You may never have put pen to paper about what's really important to you, but you definitely have core values. Have you ever been upset because someone didn't turn up on time or let you down at the last minute? If so, reliability and punctuality might be among your core values. Have you ever been annoyed because a leader wasn't honest with you or didn't deliver on a promise? Honesty might be one of your core values. Ever felt upset because a close friend prioritised someone else? Loyalty might be high on your list of core values!

This part should be fun. The following is a list of some popular core values. Take a few moments to study the grid, and circle or shade the values that are most important to you. You might take a glance and think they're all important. But what you're looking for are the ones that jump out or resonate most with who you are. You can choose as many or as few as you like.

authenticity	adventure	autonomy	accountability
animal rights	flexibility	home	tenacity
compassion	citizenship	community	contribution
creativity	curiosity	competency	courage
determination	dependability	concern for others	commitment
consistency	charity	freedom	family
faith	fairness	friendship	fun
friendliness	enthusiasm	fearlessness	equality
growth	integrity	independence	fitness
happiness	honesty	humour	human rights
influence	education	environmentalism	excellence
justice	hard work	passion	learning
kindness	knowledge	standing up for the underdog	nurturing the next generation
meaningful work	positivity	patriotism	philanthropy
leadership	love	loyalty	perseverance
openness	optimism	peace	success
religion	reputation	respect	responsibility
self-respect	service	spirituality	stability
trustworthiness	open-mindedness	reliability	social justice
wisdom	wealth	tolerance	stewardship

When you've chosen your values, write them out again below and take a good look. Reading this list should feel really affirming! It's good to know what's important to you. Now, here is a real challenge … Pick your top ten. It might take a while if you've chosen a lot. But you'll need them later on so give it your best shot.

MY TOP TEN CORE VALUES

1
....

2
....

3
....

4
....

5
....

6
....

7
....

8
....

9
....

10
....

Part 2: Living in line with your own values

I'm passionate about mental health and I've discovered something important: our wellness is dependent on living in line with our own values. If honesty is a core value for you but you're living with a secret, things may start to go downhill with your mental health. If you want to feel a sense of peace when you go to bed at night it's important to live what you believe. No one is perfect and you won't get it right every time. But raise the bar high and do your best. The benefits will speak for themselves.

Living in line with your values will also help attract the right relationships and partnerships in life (more on that later). If you know what's important to you, you're more likely to gravitate towards those who share your values. Being clear on what you care about means others will see what you're about too. Those who come into your life won't be able to ignore what matters to you. You'll weed out those who don't share your convictions. And you'll even be able to influence those around you. If ever you're feeling low or confused about where you are in life, come back to your list of core values and check that you're living in line with them. If not, a little adjustment here and there might make all the difference.

'Progress not perfection'

There's a little hypocrisy in all of us; we're only human. No one lives out their beliefs fully at all times. It's pretty inevitable at some time or other that you'll fall short of the bar you have set for yourself. We have to be careful we don't end up constantly bashing ourselves for the times we fail. If you're a very conscientious person or a bit of a perfectionist, you could actually end up making yourself miserable simply for being human. While we should try our best to live what we believe, we shouldn't get weighed down by the pressure to 'be good' and get it right 24/7.

For it is by grace you have been saved, through faith – and this is not from yourselves, it is the gift of God – not by works, so that no one can boast.

EPHESIANS 2:8–9

God's greatest gift to us is Jesus and because of Him, we get to live in God's grace. God's grace covers our mistakes, making up for the ways we fall short in life. It's important to remember that our principles and values don't make us perfect. We do our best and God carries us the rest of the way!

> Do not judge, or you too will be judged. For in the same way you judge others, you will be judged, and with the measure you use, it will be measured to you.
>
> MATTHEW 7:1–2

It's great to live in accordance with our values. When we're getting it right, it gives us a sense of well-being and peace. But when we're on our A-game, walking the talk and representing ourselves well, it's easy to begin judging others. The more we clean up our own act, the more obvious it might be that others aren't doing the same. Scripture reminds us that it's not our business to judge others. All we should be doing is thanking God for His help and doing our best. If ever we're tempted to point out someone's shortcomings, we should come back to basics and focus on our own journey.

Time to Pray

Lord, help me to know what matters to me and to live with integrity. I want to be a good example to others and of the things I care about. Help me to accept that I'm not perfect and that Your grace carries me every time

I fall short. And help me to walk in grace so that those around me feel encouraged and inspired, not judged. Amen.

Section Five

Purpose

Having purpose in life is integral to our happiness. Most of us agree that 'life is short' and in the grand scheme of things we don't have long here on earth. We don't want to feel we're just drifting aimlessly; we want our efforts to count and to feel we're here for a reason.

We find our sense of purpose in a variety of ways. We find it in the work we do and the things we create. We find purpose in our interests and passions as well as in the things we do to care for others. Some of us find our purpose when we discover what upsets us most about the world! Finding a cause to support can be our making. That sense of purpose ties into our sense of identity in a big way. And when we figure out what makes us tick, we often feel we're finding ourselves too. In this section we're going to explore:

- what gives us purpose
- how to identify what we're made for
- the role purpose plays in who we are.

What comes to mind when you think about your purpose in life? Have you got a talent or a passion? Do you have a strong conviction about something you want to change in the world? Are you excited about having your own family? These are all things in life that give us purpose.

Take a few moments now to consider what you think you're made for. Whether you have a really strong idea or no clue at all, just write whatever comes to mind ...

Part 1: What is purpose?

> The two most important days in your life are the day you are born and the day you find out why.
>
> MARK TWAIN

This quote is powerful. For those with a strong dream or clear direction, I'm sure it really resonates. But not everybody knows what they want to do in life. For lots of us there isn't a lightbulb moment. Many of us have big questions about what we're supposed to be doing or have no idea where to start. Even if we do have a specific dream or 'calling', we might wonder if we're wasting our time. We might ask questions like, *'Am I barking up the wrong tree with this job or course? Am I good enough for this?'*

When God says He has 'plans' for us, we often wish we knew what they were! The truth is, most of us need a little help and encouragement along the way. Over the next few pages, we're going to do some digging and exploration into what God says about purpose, and look at some ways we can figure out 'why we're here'.

Rosie had a difficult upbringing. She had suffered trauma in her teens and decided that, when things got better, she wanted to  be a counsellor. It felt like a huge breakthrough. But the year she enrolled for college was a tough one. She had some personal troubles and health issues, which meant she couldn't keep up with the course and had to drop out after the first term. I sat with her as she poured her heart out, tears flowing because she felt she'd missed out on a key moment in her life. I suggested she get a job in the meantime and spend some time focusing on herself.

Rosie did just that. She got a part-time job at a local restaurant. It was hard at first and she struggled to be happy about it. Waitressing was not her ideal job by any means. Taking food to tables was nothing like sitting with someone in an office, hearing their problems and offering help. She felt wasted.

But Rosie settled in to her role at the restaurant, finding new ways to enjoy it. She made time to listen to the stories of customers who dined alone. Often, she found they were struggling and just needed a listening ear. She also found that her colleagues came to her when things got tough for them. Because of what she'd been through in her life, she always had the patience to listen and offer support. This inspired her to do some training and volunteer for a church that took in vulnerable young people. There, she became a support worker. In doing so, she was able to show God's love to people who needed it.

Eventually, Rosie realised that her purpose wasn't waiting for her at the end of a degree course or in a swanky office somewhere. She was living out her purpose right where she was. She was gifted at listening, caring and pointing people towards the love of God. And she knew now she could do that amongst her friends, as a volunteer for her church or even at the restaurant where she worked.

This story is not about giving up on your education of choice. It isn't about ditching your dream. It's important to realise that **your purpose is not defined by what you do**. You can walk in your purpose wherever you are.

First, there are two main types of purpose: **personal purpose** and **shared purpose**. The dreams we have of using our gifts and talents are about

personal purpose. Shared purpose is where we fit into the bigger picture. Think of it like this: somewhere in a factory right now a worker is stitching together protective face masks. They're making a living, providing for their family and using their skill. But what they do is also serving a larger purpose: helping protect lives and fight a pandemic.

This illustrates the way we should think about purpose. What we do might help us to make a living to provide for ourselves and our families, while using the skills and gifts God has given us. But whatever we do should also serve that larger purpose—God's plan.

> For we are his workmanship, created in Christ Jesus for good works, which God prepared beforehand, that we should walk in them.
>
> EPHESIANS 2:10 ESV

This Scripture in Ephesians says that **God has created us to do good things**. Because God sees the whole picture at once and knows what needs to be done, He is able to create us specifically to do those things. In other words, God has custom-made you for the jobs He wants you to do!

YOU ARE AN ANSWER TO A PROBLEM

What if I were to tell you that you were born to be a solution? Well, it's true. This world has its fair share of issues. It's a world that's hurting in many ways and needs the light of God's truth. You were born to shine His light in a way that only you can. You were designed perfectly to illuminate your surroundings. And God inserted you into this very season. He decided that of all the moments in history, your time to live is right now. He saw the way the world would look in this age and crafted you perfectly as a solution to some of that chaos.

That doesn't mean you're going to single-handedly cure cancer or solve world hunger (although, who knows? You might!). But being God's workmanship means you have everything it takes to be someone's answered prayer. You don't have to be the cleverest person or the most creative. You don't need the best grades or the most incredible talent. But you are able to make this world brighter and more beautiful just by being you and living according to God's Word. This might seem unlikely or even impossible to you right now, but God gives us plenty of pointers on how we can find and fulfil the purposes we were born for.

WORKS, NOT WORK

Notice how in that Scripture in Ephesians it says 'works' rather than 'work'. God wants to make it clear that we are created to do more than one thing. Our purpose won't only be found in our job, even if it's our dream job. You can walk in your purpose within a variety of roles and places. This might not be what you want to hear right now. Perhaps you are desperate for a break in the music industry or for an opportunity to open in a certain field. But it's good to know that God really can use you wherever you are.

As an aspiring artist, the last thing I ever wanted to hear was *'You'd make a great teacher'* or even *'You'll make a great mum'*. I had such a strong sense that I was born to sing, I felt discouraged when people suggested I might do other things in life too. But just because I had potential in other areas didn't mean God would never open a door for me as a singer-songwriter. I taught singing for years before I landed my first major tour or made my own record.

WE ARE NOT WHAT WE DO

Doing a job that gives us a sense of purpose can help define who we are. But it's important not to get 'what we do' out of perspective. Purpose is often associated directly with our occupation. We might decide our purpose is to be a teacher, a nurse or a musician, for instance. But there is more to what we're actually made for than that. What we do connects to our purpose but it doesn't stop there. In fact, we can live a life of purpose in absolutely any job, at any stage of our lives! Purpose is less about what we do and more about how we do it. And, of course, who we do it for.

WE'RE MADE TO DO THINGS WELL

Whatever you do [whatever your task may be], work from the soul [that is, put in your very best effort], as [something done] for the Lord and not for men

COLOSSIANS 3:23 AMP

Our purpose is not only in what we do. Our purpose is to do things in a way that sets us apart. Just as loving each other should set us apart from the crowd, so should the way we work. Showing up on time, doing a great job, being helpful and willing to go the extra mile will help others see you're something special. Whether you're flipping burgers, scoring goals, writing novels or saving lives, you can bring something extra special to the world by doing it as though you are working for the King of the universe.

YOU ARE GIFTED

You are the light of the world. A town built on a hill cannot be hidden. Neither do people light a lamp and put it under a bowl. Instead they put it on its stand, and it gives light to everyone in the house. In the same way, let your light shine before others, that they may see your good deeds and glorify your Father in heaven.

MATTHEW 5:14–16

Finding your individual purpose can take a little time and work. But whether you realise it or not, there are things within you that can be useful and life-giving to others. Gifts are not just obvious things like artistic skills. Your gift might be taking care of people. It might be cleaning. It might be arguing! Or you could be super caring and patient. Those things can bring God's light into people's worlds.

DO WHATEVER YOU CAN

Whatever your hand finds to do, do it with all your might

ECCLESIASTES 9:10

Scripture tells us to 'do whatever our hand finds to do'. That means, in any season, wherever we are, we should look at what we can do and get on with it. During the pandemic, live musicians were forced to put their careers on pause. When my husband and I were unable to tour, we had to look at what God had put at our fingertips. We had a van, which was normally our touring vehicle, and Joel is a great driver, thanks to thousands of miles on the road driving us around the country for shows. Joel signed up to be a medical courier during the pandemic, delivering blood samples and tests, PPE and research documents. He continued to serve God, despite not being behind a drum kit. This is a great example of finding purpose in any season.

YOUR PURPOSE IS TO SERVE

Each of you should use whatever gift you have received to serve others, as faithful stewards of God's grace in its various forms.

1 PETER 4:10

The heart to serve others is one the major keys to success in life. The best performers understand that they're called to serve their audience; the best sports people play as though to serve their region or country. Whatever we do, we will do it best when we're serving a bigger picture.

FOCUS ON GOD'S WILL

your kingdom come, your will be done, on earth as it is in heaven.

MATTHEW 6:10

Every day is different. So it's good to begin each morning by asking God to help you do His will. God is good and He wants life to be rich, exciting and filled with good things for us. He created you for good works and those works will fit you like a glove when you do them. But we're here to fulfil God's purposes and not just our own.

YOU CAN ALWAYS LOVE SOMEONE

Do everything in love.

1 CORINTHIANS 16:14

If your life has changed because of a pandemic, a health issue or simply the sands of time, don't give up on your purpose. If you didn't have work left to do, you wouldn't still be here! You're still at work. Never forget, the most valuable thing you can add to someone's life is love itself. As long as you have the ability to love another person, you have a calling and a place in this world.

Who in your life needs to be loved? Write their name(s) below.

Part 2: Identifying your individual purpose

Now, here's the fun bit. These four short exercises can help you pin down your personal purpose. Try to write as many details as possible. This will help you see a picture emerge.

WHAT ARE YOU GOOD AT?

God actually *created* you for specific good works. So what are you naturally good at? Are you good at making people laugh? Are you good at organising? Are you a listener? A fast runner? List everything below, however insignificant you might think it to be.

WHAT DO YOU LOVE TO DO?

What makes you forget everything? My sister loves to walk her dogs. She told me, *'When I'm out with the dogs I forget all my troubles.'* Very often the things that make us happy are connected with what we're made to do. List your favourite things below.

....

....

....

....

....

....

WHAT ARE YOU NATURALLY DOING?

The things we're already doing can hint at what we're made for. The way we're living right now can reveal strengths, weaknesses, passions and talents. For instance, do you spend a lot of your time creating things? Are you always the one organising the event or planning the party? These are markers of purpose. Try to list next the things you find yourself spending time on.

WHAT DO YOU FIND YOURSELF COMPLAINING ABOUT?

A hint about our calling can often be found within what upsets us. Passion brings with it a dissatisfaction with the way things are being done. For example, nothing makes me angrier than advertising that promotes unhelpful beauty stereotypes! So I've made it a big focus in my songwriting and what I share on stage.

WHAT HAVE YOU 'FALLEN INTO'?

As irrelevant as your current job, pastime, home situation etc might seem, God is not a wasteful God. If you're praying for God's will to be done in your life, your current location and occupation are no accident. It may not be where you want to be, but God is doing something in and through you right now. How do you think God might be using you in this season?

Three ways to know you're 'on purpose'

Maybe you're wondering if what you're doing is right for you. Perhaps you're not sure if you've found your passion yet. Here are three ways to know you're in the right spot.

YOU FEEL LIKE A FISH IN WATER

You've heard the phrase *'like a fish out of water'*. We use this to describe being in an environment or role that doesn't quite fit. Feeling like a fish out of water might even seem as though your environment is squeezing the life from you. Being in the wrong job, of course, is not totally without value. But being *fully* in your lane makes you feel alive. As a songwriter, being around other songwriters and musicians makes *me* feel alive. We speak the same language and even find the same things funny. When I see my songs blessing someone I feel truly fulfilled. Pay attention to what makes you feel alive. There is purpose there.

YOU'RE LEARNING AND GROWING

Purpose to us is like plant food to plants. When we're in it, we flourish. So ask yourself, *'Am I growing? Am I a better person than I was last year? Do I feel stronger and more beautiful for doing that I'm doing? Or am I withering and feeling smaller than I should?'*

YOU'RE MAKING CONNECTIONS

Powerful, life-giving interactions are a sign we're in the right place at the right time. Do you feel you're meeting people you connect with on a heart level? Do you feel you're on the same wavelength with the people around you? Look for precious, life-giving moments in your interactions today.

Being pregnant in a pandemic was hard. I felt isolated and unable to unpack the experience with other mums because  of lockdown. And when my baby girl was born, it got even harder. I went a year without performing or sharing my story, which I love to do. Talking about faith and letting people know God loves them is my passion. But even then, I found myself unexpectedly able to do that during my pregnancy. I had two incredible experiences of sharing my story with midwives. Even in the birthing pool, I found myself sharing my testimony with a lady who was helping to deliver my baby! It was a powerful spiritual moment and it helped me realise I don't have to be on stage to operate in my gift and be 'on purpose'. I knew that, in spite of appearances, I was actually right where God wanted me to be.

Time to Pray

Instead of focusing on what we're good at and our long-term goals, the most important thing we can do is commit today to God's purposes. Let's do that now …

Lord, thank You that You custom-built me for my individual purposes. Thank You that I have a part to play in Your big picture and that there will always be things for me to do while I'm on earth. Help me have eyes to see what You're asking of me. Help me to be willing to do Your work wherever I find myself, and to love it. And please help me to discern the important connections You want me to make each day. In Jesus' name. Amen.

Section Six

The importance of relationships

> You will be the same person in five years as you are today except for the people you meet and the books you read.
>
> CHARLIE TREMENDOUS JONES

When we think about the sort of person we want to be, we should consider the type of relationships we want to have. That's what this section is all about. Perhaps the single most influential force in our lives will be the people we spend time with. If we want to evolve into something greater, we need to be intentional about our relationships.

HUMANS ARE LIKE PARROTS

It only takes spending a few hours with a small child to see that we learn by watching others. Within a handful of short months, a newborn will begin mimicking sounds and facial expressions. Before you know it, new babies will be copying entire phrases. This human way of learning never stops. We can't help absorbing language and habits from others.

HUMANS ARE LIKE CHAMELEONS

Ever spent time in another town and noticed the trends are different? We are influenced by our communities more than we realise. When I was sixteen, everyone in my friendship group dressed a certain way. We shared clothes and even cut our hair into the same style. It's not unusual to slowly morph into the people we spend the most time with.

HUMANS ARE INFLUENCERS

We've already done our social media crash course, but we didn't really unpack the power of the 'influencer'. Influencers use their platforms to promote products, brands and other sorts of content. They're primarily known for what they do online, sharing advice, tips and product recommendations. The thing is, we are actually *all* influencers whether we realise it or not.

Ever ordered in a restaurant and watched the next table go for the same thing moments later? Or perhaps you've been shopping and seen someone grab the same garment you're carrying? You are an influencer and science supports the theory. All the data says you're far more likely to choose something from a menu if someone on your table chooses it first. Bottom line? You might be more likely to choose things because your peers do.

We're created to be in relationship

> The LORD God said, 'It is not good for the man to be alone.'
>
> GENESIS 2:18

We need relationship. It's not a luxury, it's an essential part of life. Children need touch and connection to develop. Adults are just as needy. But the quality of our relationships matters. Having chaotic or toxic relationships can hinder our development and our enjoyment of life. In this section, we're going to take a broad look at the main relationships in our lives and how they affect who we become. Within our lives we have many relationships to manage. But the main ones are:

family

friends

romantic partners

work colleagues

ourselves

God

A lot of the time we focus on the relationships that demand our attention most, namely family, friends, partners and colleagues. But actually, the most important relationships are the ones we have with ourselves and with God. We're going to do some exploring of those in a moment.

Have a look at the list on the previous page. How are your relationships within it going? Why not take a moment to consider each category and ask yourself how things are looking. Feel free to write notes next to each one, bringing anything to mind that might be bothering you.

What God says

> Love the LORD your God with all your heart and with all your soul and with all your strength.
>
> DEUTERONOMY 6:5

Your relationship with God is your most important one. 'Love the LORD your God with all your heart and with all your soul' is the very first commandment. God is not insecure. He doesn't ask us to love Him because He is greedy or needs the attention. God is not a bearded man on a cloud looking for affirmation. He is everything good, wise and powerful. So why does He command us to love Him above all else?

GOD'S LOVE SETS THE STANDARD

For God so loved the world that he gave his one and only Son, that whoever believes in him shall not perish but have eternal life.

JOHN 3:16

God's love sets the standard for all the other sorts of love in our lives. He knows that when we are living in a healthy relationship with Him, it helps us to do everything else better. When you plug in to God, you will be a better friend. When you seek God's heart for your life, you will pick your partner more thoughtfully. When you know what you mean to God, you'll have a better idea of when you're being treated right and when you're not. When you know and believe the depth of God's love for you, you can truly begin to love yourself and others. In short, knowing what you're worth and living out of that knowledge will change your life and your relationships forever.

GOD IS YOUR POWER

I am the true vine, and my Father is the vinedresser. Every branch in me that does not bear fruit he takes away, and every branch that does bear fruit he prunes, that it may bear more fruit.

JOHN 15:1–2 ESV

I love to see charging points for electric cars at service stations. So futuristic! Plugging in to God is like a car plugging in to one of those charging points. It refuels us for the journey of life. Regularly spending time with God gives us perspective. It brings our hearts into line with His and keeps us healthy. If we can live in an intimate and healthy relationship with our Creator, everything else will flow from this.

Working on your relationship with God

So how can we deepen our relationship with God? Here are three quick ways to reconnect ...

BOOK A DATE WITH JESUS

Okay, this may sound a little 'cringe', but a date with Jesus can really get things back on track. It doesn't have to involve sitting in a church or even having a Bible open. Both these things can be helpful but it can actually be whatever makes you feel best connected to the Creator. For me, that's a sunset walk and some funky house music! I totally feel my heart open and my eyes lift to heaven. For you, it might be hanging out in your garden, walking your dog, rock climbing, dancing or even skateboarding. Any place you feel the freedom to open your heart is good enough. Some people even go for a whole holiday with God. It can be truly life-changing. So do yourself a favour and book a date with Jesus!

Date ideas here:

HONEST CONVERSATION

Just like any relationship, communication is key in our relationship with God. Sometimes we bottle things up that we're annoyed or upset about. Or we just forget to catch up! Any relationship can break down when we forget to talk. So, if you feel brave enough next time you're in a quiet place, just begin to say things to God out loud. It might feel odd to begin with but it will get easier.

Conversation points here:

REMINISCE ABOUT THE GOOD TIMES

If you've got friends you've known for years, you probably find yourself chatting about old times when you see each other. Shared memories create a bond and help you stay connected. If you're struggling to feel connected with God, perhaps take a minute to remember a time when you did. When did you last feel spiritual? When did you last feel thankful about something God was doing for you? Remember the good times. It can really keep you together.

Recall the last time you felt spiritually good here:

....

....

....

....

....

Part 2: Your relationship with yourself

> Do you not know that your bodies are temples of the Holy Spirit, who is in you, whom you have received from God? You are not your own; you were bought at a price. Therefore honour God with your bodies.
>
> 1 CORINTHIANS 6:19–20

Our bodies, minds and souls are connected and it's important to take care of all three. It's vital to take care of the body God gave us because it's a gift and is packaging for the Spirit. Scripture says, because we were bought by Jesus on the cross, we actually don't belong to ourselves anymore; we belong to Him. We need to take care of what belongs to God. He thought it was precious enough to give His life for. We need to treat it as though it's that valuable.

Be a good friend to yourself

If you really keep the royal law found in Scripture, 'Love your neighbour as yourself,' you are doing right.

JAMES 2:8

The Bible says to love our neighbours as ourselves. That means we have to love ourselves first! But it's not always easy. We often find ourselves putting others first or naturally presuming they're more important than we are. As believers, we're called to consider others but that doesn't mean we should neglect or abuse ourselves. We're not much good to anyone if we let ourselves become spiritually and mentally overwhelmed.

When you settle down to enjoy a flight, the attendant will announce, *'In the case of an emergency, fit your oxygen mask before helping others.'* You may love the people around you so much, you'll do anything to support them. But don't forget to attend to your own needs. When you're kind to yourself, you have more to give.

To be truly healthy and happy, we need to treat ourselves the way we would treat a best friend. All too often, we spend all our kindness on others and give ourselves the hardest time. We encourage our friends and berate ourselves. If we are to have successful relationships long-term, we need to work on the relationship we have with ourselves.

Three ways to love yourself better

SEEK HEALING

Life can leave us in a bit of a mess sometimes. Things happen that hurt or even break us. It's not a bad thing to reach out and ask for help. There are many ways to do this. We can seek therapy via the NHS. We can ask our Christian friends to pray with or for us. We can use mental wellness apps to spend time being still, mindful or peaceful. If you have deep trauma in your life, you may need specialist counselling. There is no shame in any of these things. The best thing you can do for the people in your life is to become whole and healed.

HAVE TIME FOR YOU (AND STICK TO THE PLAN)

It's not always easy to make time for ourselves. There are so many things to do and often many people who want a slice of our day. By the time you've finished all your chores, done any work you need to do for school or your job, seen your friends and remembered everybody's special occasions, there can be little time left for you. So schedule it. Make yourself a promise to visit your favourite place or take time just to browse online. I love online shopping! So I make time to sit with a drink and look at clothes on my laptop a couple of times a week after my baby is asleep. It does me the world of good.

BUY YOURSELF A GIFT

Speaking of online shopping, it's okay to treat yourself now and then. It can give you a real boost to stick on a new shirt or slather yourself in brand new body cream. You buy gifts for people you love, so why not buy something for yourself? Next time you have a spare fiver, do it!

Part 3: Your relationships with others

When it comes to the other relationships in our lives, they can be broken down into two main categories: **the relationships we choose** and **the relationships we can't choose**. We tend to choose our friends and romantic partners. We don't get to choose the families we're born or adopted into and we don't usually get to choose our classmates or workmates. So in this section, we're going to look at two main things:

- How to choose the right relationships.
- How to manage the relationships we can't choose.

The relationships we can't choose

FAMILY

Boy, families can be tricky. I'd hasten to add *all* families are tricky if you get up close. I've never come across a family who didn't have their share of struggles, secrets and problems. People are complicated and families are full of them! Plus, it's true: the ones we love are often the ones who hurt us most. Our 'nearest and dearest' know exactly which buttons to push to drive us completely up the wall!

Family stuff can have a massive impact on our personal development and sense of identity. If we're abused or rejected by a family member it can be deeply traumatic. Wounds from those super-close relationships are often the hardest to recover from. It's important we make room to deal with those hurts.

FAMILY FALLOUTS

If I had a fiver for everyone I know who has suffered a major family fallout, I could probably buy a new car! I've even had fallouts within my own family, despite all our best intentions. Things happen. People make mistakes, disagree and bottle up their true feelings. It's upsettingly common to fall out with a family member and it can make life very messy and painful.

WHAT CAN I DO ABOUT A FAMILY FALLOUT?

First, it's important to say, we can't always fix a family fallout single-handedly. Some things are outside our control. People might choose to walk away from us or remove themselves from family life. Sometimes people won't accept an apology or offer the apology we deserve. We can't control what others do but we can decide how we will respond.

HAVE PEACE

If it is possible, as far as it depends on you, live at peace with everyone.

ROMANS 12:18

The people in your family may have struggles or make choices you don't like. They may have different beliefs or values to you. You might feel you're always the one who makes the effort in certain family relationships. But whatever the issue (unless you're suffering abuse), it's usually best to keep the peace. It's not always what we feel like doing but it leads to the most workable environment and preserves relationships.

HAVE PATIENCE

Always be humble and gentle. Be patient with each other, making allowance for each other's faults because of your love.

EPHESIANS 4:2 NLT

Patience is your best friend when it comes to family life. See how it says in Ephesians, *'Always be **humble** and **gentle***' (my emphasis). We could write a book on those two words alone! Being humble means being prepared to come down off your high horse, even when you're right (or feel you are). And being gentle means doing your best to curb your aggression and sassiness.

I've always been pretty good at arguing. But when it comes to family, it's not always a good thing. What's the use in winning an argument if it means losing a relationship in the process? Notice that the Scripture also refers to *'each other's faults'*. That means you have faults too. We all have them and we all need a little grace now and again.

HAVE BOUNDARIES

Simply let your 'Yes' be 'Yes,' and your 'No,' 'No.'

MATTHEW 5:37 BSB

Boundaries are important. Decide what yours are and stick to them without guilt. For example, if you have a family member who always shows up two hours late for coffee, it's okay to decide you'll only wait an hour! Putting things like that in place can relieve a lot of frustration and help family members to adjust their expectations of you.

FORGIVE

Be kind and compassionate to one another, forgiving each other, just as in Christ God forgave you.

EPHESIANS 4:32

There's a lot to be said for turning the page and starting over, and it really is possible. My family is very verbal. We all have a tendency to say things we don't mean when we get upset. But we have discovered that we can always come back to one another, no matter what has been said. Words have the power to give and take life, so we really shouldn't be careless with them. But if ever we are, wiping the slate clean is always an option. Yes, people can be super hurtful. But God forgave us, so it's good for us to practise forgiveness too.

Time to Pray

Are you struggling with a loved one? Is a sibling or parent driving you crazy? Or have you got a deeper issue with someone in your life who closed a door on you? Let's bring that to God right now.

Lord, thank You for the grace and forgiveness over my life. I'm so grateful that You always keep the door open for me, even when I've been careless in my words or actions. Help me have grace and patience for those in my life who stretch me. Teach me to live in peace with others as much as possible. Amen.

The relationships you choose—your 'tribe'

A man is known by the company he keeps.[4]

AESOP

Some of the most significant relationships in our lives are the ones we choose. Friendships can make or break us. It's good to recognise when a friendship has run its course, stopped being good for us or even become toxic. Some friends come into our lives for just a season while others stay with us for life. The bottom line when it comes to friendships is that they should bring out the best in us. Choosing the voices and influences in our world is crucial to who we become.

How is your friendship circle right now? Do you have people you connect with? Do you feel you can trust and depend upon your friends? Or do some friendships drag you down and leave you feeling drained? We're going to spend a little time now reflecting on the friends in our lives.

Use the next five minutes to write down some names of friends and a little about what they mean to you.

....

....

....

....

....

Five signs a friendship is good for you

YOU CAN BE YOURSELF

When you find people you connect with, it's like finding your 'tribe'. But if you feel you have to put on a front or be 'fake' around certain friends, they're probably not your people. Friends don't have to be the same as us but they *should* love us for who we are. Healthy friendships are safe zones where we can speak our minds and be our true selves. Pretending to be someone we're not can lead to making choices we wouldn't ideally make.

THEY LEAVE YOU FEELING 'LIGHTER'

How do you feel after spending time with your friends? Do you feel a weight has been lifted or as though you've absorbed all their drama? It's good to talk and offload together. But if a friend leaves you feeling drained or 'heavier' than when you arrived, it might be a 'toxic' friendship. Toxic friendships are a one-way street. You end up doing all the listening, all the supporting and pretty much all the work. Healthy relationships are reciprocal.

YOU'RE ON THE SAME PAGE

This is where seasonal friendships come into play. Sometimes we make friends because they make sense at the time. You might have the same passing interests as someone or have mutual friends. Often people we work or learn with are seasonal friends. But when the season changes you might find you're drifting apart. If you're not on the same page as a friend anymore, hanging out together may feel a bit like a waste of time. If being with that person keeps you stuck in old habits, it could be holding you back. For instance, if you made a friend on a night out but no longer want to go out drinking, your shared interest has expired! Staying friends with that person could keep you in a lifestyle you no longer want.

YOU LEARN FROM ONE ANOTHER

A good friend has something to offer just by being who they are. They have a perspective that teaches you something about the world or about the way others think. I'm a believer and have close friends who are atheists. Because the friendships are loving and respectful, they help all of us to understand the world a little better.

THEY TELL YOU THE TRUTH

It's not a great feeling when someone tells you your skirt is tucked into your knickers or you have something in your teeth! But we need to know those things and they *always* sound better coming from a friend. A good friend won't sit on the sidelines and watch you make a mistake. A friend who really cares will tell you the truth when you're out of line and be honest when they're concerned for you. If you have a friend who only says what you want to hear, there's a chance they're really not all that good for you.

Spend time with the wise and you will become wise, but the friends of fools will suffer.

PROVERBS 13:20 NCV

Aim high with your friendship choices. By aiming high, I don't mean just befriend the most popular person you can find. I mean look to form friendships with people who inspire and speak life into you. Look for qualities like loyalty, honesty, reliability and vision for the future. Find the people who are on your wavelength and connect with your real interests. Then do your best to be a good friend to them too.

> ## An honest answer is a sign of true friendship.
>
> PROVERBS 24:26 GNT

Don't be tempted to walk away from the people in your life who lovingly advise you. I'm not talking about people who criticise or belittle you constantly; that's not healthy. But a friend who says things like, *'Maybe we should get an early one tonight—we have that exam tomorrow'* is probably a keeper.

So you see, friendships are a serious thing. When you consider who you want to be in five years, understand that your friends will help to shape that person. Has anyone in particular come to mind as you've been reading this section, or have you reached a point in a friendship where you're beginning to pull in separate directions? Let's pray about that now …

Lord, help me to be strong and wise about those I spend my time with. Help me to be brave and decisive when it comes to friendship. I only want to be around people who help me become the person I'm meant to be. In Jesus' name. Amen.

The relationships you choose: your 'person'

You've now given some serious thought to your beliefs, values and purpose in life. Hopefully you're building a lovely, clear picture in your mind of who you are and who you want to become. But if having a life partner is a part of that vision, you need to make sure that person is incredible; someone with a pretty clear direction in life so you can know your hearts both line up. You deserve a partner who'll encourage you to be your best self and step into all that God has for you.

After following Jesus, the partner you choose might be the most important decision you ever make.

Nothing will define the course of your future more than the person you marry. Choosing or even finding that person isn't always easy though and we have no control over when it will happen. So in this section, we'll be exploring why choosing the right person is so important and why compromising isn't worth it.

Is there a right/wrong person for me?

There's a fab scripture in Corinthians that applies brilliantly to the dating game: *'"Everything is permissible for me," but not everything is beneficial'* (1 Cor. 6:12 BSB).

For me, this a really solid principle to live by. In the actual passage, Paul is talking about food traditions and what believers should do. He is making it clear that our concern shouldn't be what we're *allowed* to do—it's not about what we can get away with. We need to focus on doing what's good for us.

Being a follower of Jesus is not about following some strict diet or code. Faith is about relationship, partnership, discipleship and potential—not keeping some bearded guy in the sky happy with you! The God of the universe knows your deepest desires and how to help you get there.

Think of God's guidance like a recipe. Recipes are not about rules; they're about nutrition and flavour. Following a recipe guarantees a meal that will taste great and fill us up. Scripture is God's recipe book for our fulfilment. There is always room for our own creativity and flare but He knows that if we follow His steps we'll get great results.

When it comes to dating, we are free to do whatever we like. But not every choice will take us in the direction of our dreams. Not every relationship will help us lead our best lives or become the people we want to be. Partnering with someone who is actually *good* for us is the best way to go.

Why do we choose the wrong person?

There are tons of reasons why we might get involved with someone who isn't right for us. Here are just a few:

- Feeling lonely.

- Desiring 'connection'.

- Because it's convenient.

- We're looking for a little fun or distraction.

- The person ticks some of the boxes but fails to tick some majorly important ones, like sharing our love of family life or our beliefs.

- Being under pressure from the other person to get involved.

- Mistaking chemistry for compatibility.

Chemistry versus compatibility

Love is a drug. Feeling all the 'feels' when you look at someone is a seriously potent natural high. There's really nothing like meeting someone, realising there's chemistry and watching it all unfold.

When you start to fall in love, your brain releases chemicals like adrenaline, dopamine, and oxytocin. These chemicals light up the brain's receptors, making us crave more contact with that person. In essence these chemicals actually cause a temporary addiction to the person we're falling for.

The infatuation stage can make you lose your senses a bit, which can be a wonderful part of the adventure. We might end up trying new things, going to new places or even moving our whole lives to be together. But if you get swept up in all those chemicals with the wrong person, you could end up getting hurt, side-tracked or pulled away from the things that matter to you.

We can't always rely on the way we *feel* about a person (especially in the beginning) to tell us if that person will be right for us. A spark is important for sure. But compatibility is so much more important than chemistry long-term.

Partnership is power

Chemistry is useful when starting a relationship. Those potent chemicals help cultivate the motivation and commitment needed to get things off the ground. But there's no use being bonded and committed to the wrong person. If we allow attraction to fog our judgement, we can end up wasting time and experiencing a lot of heartache. We also risk finding that when the chemicals level out, there's not much left to work with.

Ultimately, if we want a *great* life partner—someone we can eventually start a family and do the adventure of life with—we need to be intentional from day one.

As I write this, Joel and I have been married twelve years this September (together for fifteen). He is an incredible guy, more  than I ever could have asked for. But he's very different from anyone else I've ever dated and it wasn't obvious at first that we'd end up getting married. Later in the journal, I'll tell you more about how we got together and what happened afterwards, but for the sake of this section, I'm just going to tell you how I knew he was 'my person'.

Before I met Joel I'd been in a few relationships that weren't great for me (more on that later too). I used to go for the 'centre of attention' types. But Joel had more of a laid-back energy. When he asked me out for coffee, I didn't expect much connection as we were so different. But what set Joel apart from the get-go was a quiet certainty about what he wanted in life. He was a pastor's kid with a church background and a strong faith. He was also a drummer in an up-

and-coming band and loved music. Even on the first date, it was obvious something was different. He was clear about his feelings and intentions from the start. It sounds intense but he was so relaxed that I felt a peace about giving things a try. We took it very slowly and I definitely had my doubts in the beginning. But we shared the same convictions and values. We both knew the kind of life we wanted. We had a similar level of faith and were both prepared to go on an adventure.

Aside from that, it just sort of … worked! The first couple of years weren't totally perfect as we both still had a ton of maturing to do. But we built the relationship on good foundations and knew it was right to stick together. God has honoured that commitment and revealed year-on-year just how well suited we are. From partnership, passion has blossomed and love has deepened. We make a strong team and our relationship is getting better all the time.

Sometimes 'our person' is not who we're expecting. But fire really can ignite from firm foundations and friendship. True compatibility comes from attraction, shared values and willingness to grow. A mutual commitment to meeting each other's needs, to learning and choosing God's ways over our own, make for a powerful partnership.

Being single is better than being with the wrong person

I can vouch for this. Being with someone who isn't right for you is *not* better than being alone. Sometimes we think it is, especially when we see our friends coupled up and happy. But nothing makes you feel lonelier than being with the wrong person. Being with someone who doesn't appreciate you or who isn't on the same page within the relationship can leave you broken-hearted. The wrong relationship will always have you pulling in opposite directions. It will never progress or become what you want it to be. It can also:

- cause confusion about where your life is going
- prevent you from reaching your potential and goals
- keep you from finding a relationship that would make you truly happy.

All these things subtract from your life. 'Your person' will not only add to you, they'll help you to multiply! The right relationship accelerates your growth and compounds your purpose.

How do I choose the right person?

If you refer back to the stuff on friendship, you'll find a lot of relevant pointers there. But here are some helpful tips for choosing a relationship that not only adds to you but multiplies you …

FIGURE OUT YOUR 'NON-NEGOTIABLES' AND STICK TO THEM

Non-negotiables are things you don't want to compromise on in a relationship. You could even say they're things you shouldn't compromise on because they are integral to who you are and where you're going.

DON'T MAKE A SHOPPING LIST

Ideally, non-negotiables shouldn't be things like hair colour! If you create a shopping list of surface features you could miss an awesome person. A guy with a six-pack might get your pupils dilating but won't necessarily guarantee your 'happy ever after'! (Side note: wanting to live a healthy lifestyle is a good quality though and could be non-negotiable for you if that is a part of who you are.) When it comes to finding a soulmate, don't 'guess who'-style eliminate people based on surface traits alone. Don't rule someone out because of their build or their taste in movies (you can always have movie nights with your mates instead). You don't need to agree on everything or even have the same kind of personality. The things you're not going to sway on should be things that are truly central for your happiness.

Going back to your core values could help with

this. Do you want children? Do you want a partner who shares your beliefs? Do you need to laugh every day? Do you need a partner who is willing to travel? Take five minutes now to think of five things you won't compromise on in a life partner.

MY FUTURE LIFE PARTNER SHOULD ...
Examples:

- be honest and have integrity
- want to have children
- have a strong faith
- share my love of music
- put me and our family first.

Here are some great Scriptures to use on your dating journey. Why not choose one, write it out and put it somewhere visible in your home? Remind  yourself regularly to aim for the best relationship God has for you.

COMMON PURPOSE

'It's better to have a partner than go it alone. Share the work, share the wealth. And if one falls down, the other helps, but if there's no one to help, tough!' (Eccl. 4:9–10 MSG).

CONNECTION

'Also, if two lie down together, they will keep warm. But how can one keep warm alone? Though one may be overpowered, two can defend themselves. A cord of three strands is not quickly broken' (Eccl. 4:11–12).

INTEGRITY

'The righteous lead blameless lives; blessed are their children after them' (Prov. 20:7).

Finding your forever person is a big deal. If a relationship is something you want, it should be someone who not only adds to your life but helps you to multiply in every way. Let's give all this to God right now.

Lord, I don't want to waste my time or the life You've given me with someone who doesn't see my value or understand my potential. Help my heart to become ready for the right person and help that person to be ready for me too. Keep me from compromising because of loneliness or boredom. Teach me to be patient and to trust in Your perfect timing. Amen.

Section Seven

Beauty, envy and insecurity

Welcome, stunning one! This section is all about you and your beauty. We'll look at what beauty is, how we feel about it and how we can embrace it. We'll also give ourselves a reminder of some of the things that shape our ideas about beauty. Focusing on the way we look is nothing new. Beauty has been talked about and celebrated since the dawn of time. Even the Bible contains beauty references. But there are lots of pitfalls to exploring beauty, especially when it comes to seeing and appreciating our own.

Honesty First

Do you feel beautiful? How do you feel about your body and face on a daily basis? Use the space below to write some thoughts.

Part 1:
Being beautiful

Mirror, Mirror: smashing our unhealthy beliefs about beauty

Ever noticed that in fairytales it's always the beautiful princess and not the 'ugly step-sister' who gets the guy? We learn in very subtle ways from childhood that physical beauty is everything. We're also taught to be in constant competition with one another, especially when it comes to our looks. In the story of Snow White, a younger, more beautiful princess drives the queen crazy with jealousy. She simply can't handle another girl being *the fairest of them all* and promptly banishes her competition from the kingdom! I love a good story but these narratives haven't helped us form healthy views around beauty. They've taught us to place a high value on so-called 'good looks' and always to be on the lookout for our competition in others.

Unfortunately, there is a grain of truth within these fairytales. People who look a certain way *do* seem to get the most attention within pop culture. The entertainment industry favours certain stereotypes of beauty and we still see a lot of ageism in TV, film and music.

But in real life, beauty is far more diverse and exotic. Different cultures embrace different beauty ideals and trends. One culture may prefer a leaner physique while another might favour curves. Other periods in history demonstrate different ideals too. The sixties saw more slender models rising to fame, while later decades saw the return of curvier stars. But people are attracted to all sorts of looks, shapes and sizes so there really is no such thing as the 'perfect face or body'. There are simply different trends and different tastes.

Beauty and advertising: the seven deadly sins of marketing

Advertising sells us a lie that if we 'look better', we'll be happier. We're constantly fed a narrative that, with the right products, we'll get more attention, make more friends and have more fun. The right lipstick or perfume might even help us attract true love and sail off into the sunset. **But all this is just clever marketing.** If you look closely, you'll see these 'seven deadly sins' in advertising on a daily basis:

1. **Lust** – Making products look sexy or claiming the product will make us sexier.

2. **Gluttony** – Stimulating our appetites with enticing food imagery. For example, steaming gravy being poured over a juicy roast

dinner, or chocolate sauce oozing from a pudding. Mmmm …

3. **Greed** – Making us want more. It's not enough to have a car. We need a *better* car. It's not enough to have a new phone. We need the *newest* phone.

4. **Envy** – Subtle suggestions that a product will make us more popular or the 'envy' of others.

5. **Pride** – The suggestion that owning or using a product will make us a better person in some way (ethical brands, for example).

6. **Sloth** – Selling us things that promise to make life easier.

7. **Wrath** – Exposing us to images or information that makes us angry. Believe it or not, this is really common, especially on social media platforms.

The seven deadly sins, by the way, aren't listed in the Bible; that's a common misconception. But all these tactics target our potential weak spots and advertisers know it. Making us feel we're not good enough encourages us to part with our cash. Insecurity is making a lot of people very rich.

Personal grooming has always been a thing and it's not all bad. Taking a little time to enjoy the way we look can give us a feel-good boost. Even the Bible refers to beauty treatments in the book of Esther. But advertising means that a whole industry now *'cashes in'* on our dissatisfaction with ourselves and envy of others. According to a recent report, the global cosmetics industry generated $380.2 billion in 2019, and is expected to reach $463.5 billion by 2027. Lots of us are spending a good portion of our income on beauty, and mental-health stats suggest it's not making us happier. Even those within the industry have high rates of anxiety and depression. In other words, being more stereotypically beautiful doesn't actually help us to *feel* more beautiful.

Six ways to actually feel more beautiful

EMBRACE YOUR FACE

You are beautiful in a way no one else is! Your face reflects your heritage, your unique DNA and your personality. Variety keeps our attention, so making your face look like every other face on Instagram actually makes you less noticeable! Instead of trying to look like the other faces, look at what makes yours special. Look at your unique skin tone and eye colour. Pay attention to your scars and freckles. Look affectionately at the shape of your nose, cheeks and chin. These things distinguish you from other people. Enjoy them!

MARKET YOURSELF

In order to become instantly more beautiful, all we have to do is decide that we are. I know it sounds a bit nuts, but the way we carry ourselves changes the way we're perceived by others. The industry ideals of beauty are mostly down to marketing. So become your own marketing guru and smile as though you're on a billboard! Hold yourself like the beauty you are and that's what others will see.

ZOOM OUT

Beauty marketing fixates on individual features of the face and body. Just imagine a lipstick advert for a moment. Ads like these zoom in on the lips, pulling our focus away from the face as a whole. We can become obsessed with the details of our own faces instead of appreciating the bigger picture. **We start to look at our faces as projects.** A cosmetic surgeon once said, *'You can give a person the perfect nose and ruin a face in the process.'* So maybe your lips are a little thin. Maybe you have a little bump on the bridge of your nose. But you're more than just a collection of parts. You are a whole picture.

TAKE CARE OF YOURSELF

Self-care promotes natural beauty. It's amazing what good sleep, hydration and regular exercise will do for you. Not only will these things improve your appearance, they'll vastly improve the way you feel about yourself too. When you're feeling fresh and sharp your natural beauty will shine through.

STOP COMPARING YOURSELF TO OTHERS

Ever walked through a beautiful garden and admired the flowers or stopped to look in a bakery window? Variety is beautiful. Just because someone else has a great look, it doesn't diminish yours. Think of yourself as an exotic flower or a lush caramel slice! Your unique colours and flavours only make you more appealing.

BE KIND

A kind smile is like water in the desert. If you show someone kindness you will be beautiful to them. The most beautiful people I have ever met were those taking care of leprosy-affected homeless people in India. Their compassion and tenderness to vulnerable strangers literally lit them up. Don't be tempted to swap your sparkly smile for a moody pout. It may get the likes on Insta but it won't leave any sort of lasting impression on the people you meet.

When I was sixteen, a record producer told me I wasn't pretty enough to be a pop star. At the time I had written and produced about sixty

songs of my own, and had just travelled six hours on a coach only to be told I was ordinary looking! Those words had a deep impact on me and for years I tried to change my appearance to be more acceptable to the music industry. But the more I dieted and dyed my hair, the less beautiful I felt. Years on, I've found my purpose and overcome the lies. I forged a career in music without changing my looks. And, thanks to my faith, I finally love what I see in the mirror.

But nothing adjusted my perspective more than having a baby girl. Looking at Ozma, it's hard to imagine her ever feeling insecure. I find myself staring at her when she sleeps because she's so perfect. When she wakes, I can't wait to see her smile because it literally takes my breath away. Babies are the most beautiful creatures imaginable without even trying.

When we see a baby, we see a miracle. Although there are seven billion people on the earth, we still find every child incredible! I thought that when I became a mum, I'd be itching to teach my child all about body confidence. But now I have Ozma, I find myself not even wanting to mention it because I don't want seeds of doubt in her mind. She is GLORIOUS and I want her to be as happy throughout her whole life as I am when I look at her.

The truth is, God feels exactly the same about each of us. The world feeds us a message that we're supposed to be a certain thing. But we can't ever improve on what God has designed. So I've put together a few thoughts for my little girl. As you read them, try to imagine you're hearing God's voice speaking over you ...

Love your body. Respect it. Take care of it. It's powerful, beautiful and unlike any other. But while you respect it, know that you are not your body; you are simply in it. It is your vehicle for adventures in this world. Enjoy having it. Don't let it have you. Don't give more attention to it than it deserves. If you focus too hard on making it perfect you will miss so much of what it can experience. Don't make it your idol. Don't make it your greatest project. If you do, you will never be happy because it will never match your illusions.

You're going to see thousands of pictures of bodies that impress you and you will compare yourself to them. Please know that these pictures are just constructions; they are not reality. You are reality and infinitely beautiful. We have a tendency to appreciate beauty that is different to our own that bit more. Try to remember that everyone tends to want what they don't have. Leaner girls admire curvier girls. Girls with bigger boobs often wish they were smaller. Brunettes often wish they were blondes and vice versa.

Changing hair colours and being creative with our looks can be fun—just like dressing up can be fun. But looking for happiness by altering your appearance is like looking for the end of a rainbow; you will never find it there. As close as you may get to so-called 'perfection', it will always be just out of reach. Focus on seeing the beauty of the rainbow right where you are. Try to see yourself the way you might if you were someone else.

Above all, try to remember that whatever you feel about your body, I love it. In fact, I made it. And when I saw it for the first time I could hardly believe its absolute perfection. Enjoy it for the gift that it is. And always remember you are a gift to me.

Part 2: Beauty and love

There are three main reasons we want to look our best:

- For ourselves.
- For the impression we make on others.
- To be attractive to a partner.

Biologically speaking, we do have some programming in that final area. It's natural to want to be attractive to a potential mate. But it's a lie that you *have* to look a certain way to find 'your person'. **Attraction is about connection.** Being your true self is the best way to attract the right person.

Outward appearance only counts for so much. Roald Dahl got it right in *The Twits* when he wrote:

If a person has ugly thoughts, it begins to show on the face. You can have a wonky nose and a crooked mouth and a double chin and stick-out teeth, but if you have good thoughts it will shine out of your face like sunbeams and you will always look lovely.[5]

This is very true. We probably all know someone who impressed us with their looks to begin with but turned out not to be so lovely later on. The opposite is also true. We can meet a person who doesn't stand out at first but gets more attractive the longer we know them. The heart really does shine through over time.

Beauty is more than skin deep

There's a reason rock stars and comedians are attractive (and it's not just about money and fame). Talent is attractive. And so is humour. The ingredients for long-term attraction lie within the person you are. Your kindness and sense of fun are more desirable long-term than your body parts! These are the traits that connect us on a deeper level and 'your person' will appreciate them more than anyone else.

You are altogether beautiful, my darling; there is no flaw in you.

SONG OF SONGS 4:7

This Scripture from Song of Songs is super interesting. Was it really true? Was there really 'no flaw' in the person described here? It's unlikely. No one is perfect after all! It seems to me that what God is saying through this passage is 'love is blind'. It's not only the 'flawless'

people on Instagram who fall in love. Love makes us appear 'flawless' to the one who loves us.

> Charm is deceptive, and beauty is fleeting; but a woman who fears the LORD is to be praised.
>
> PROVERBS 31:30

This is also a way of God saying the surface things will lose their appeal pretty quickly. Eventually even perfect skin and hair will age. But having a solid foundation of character and faith will make for a long and happy relationship—at least where both people are committed.

Reflect and Reframe

At this point in the section, let's take a moment to reflect on the beautiful things about ourselves. Do you have a good sense of humour? Are you caring? Do you make a darn good lemon drizzle cake? Can you thrash your mates at pool? All these things can be super attractive! So celebrate them now.

Part 3: Envy and insecurity

Feeling envious of others can make life pretty miserable. It prevents us enjoying our own beauty and can even affect our opportunities. When I was doing lots of auditions, I often used to look at the other girls in the audition queue and feel insecure. If I didn't do well in the audition, I would tend to put it down to not being as attractive as some of the other candidates. My faith has really helped me to reframe that belief.

Imitation is limitation

When we admire others we often try to be like them but imitation is limitation. If we morph into those we admire, we actually turn down the vibrancy of our own beauty. In this world, God made room for you. He decided there was a need for your unique and powerful form of beauty. Think of a woman or man you admire. Sure, the world might be better with them in it but it doesn't need another one of them!

Beauty is lifting others

Insecurity can be pretty ugly. If we become insecure about someone, we might find ourselves willing them to fail or delighting when they do. There's nothing beautiful about that. Beautiful people lift others. If ever we feel jealous, threatened or insecure it's important to take hold of those thoughts before they take hold of us. Stand confidently in your own beauty and celebrate the beauty you see in others. God has enough favour to bless all His kids. We don't need to worry about someone else stealing our opportunities or our glory. No one can take what God has set aside for you.

Beauty is a job

If ever you feel inadequate because models look so immaculate, remember it's a model's job to look perfect. If it was *your* job to look perfect you probably would too! In life, we can pretty much achieve whatever we set out to do, so long as we're prepared to do the work and make the sacrifices. If you really want to look like an Instagram model, you probably can. But if that's not your focus, don't sweat it. You more than likely have other things to think about and that's okay.

Crush on who you're going to be

We often crush on other women and their beauty. But here's a thought. How about making 'future you' your crush? How about setting the bar at where you will be when you reach your potential? Look forward to reflecting God's glory more than ever before. Your confidence and ease with yourself can grow. Your patience, kindness and capacity for love can increase.

They say beauty fades with time but beauty actually becomes more vibrant when we grow spiritually. You can find out what fits you, mind, body and soul, and learn to wear it well.

Your beauty should not come from outward adornment, such as elaborate hairstyles and the wearing of gold jewellery or fine clothes. Rather, it should be that of your inner self, the unfading beauty of a gentle and quiet spirit

1 PETER 3:3–4

This is a commonly misunderstood verse. God isn't telling us not to wear nice clothes or do our hair! This verse is reminding us that what we wear isn't what makes us beautiful. The person beneath is where the beauty truly lies. True beauty comes from the kindness and peace within us.

See how the flowers of the field grow. They do not labour or spin. Yet I tell you that not even Solomon in all his splendour was dressed like one of these.

MATTHEW 6:28–29

Trying to keep up with the latest trends and expectations can be exhausting. God is reminding us in this Scripture that our natural beauty is enough. We don't need to fret over our wardrobes or have washboard abs to be attractive. Even the most expensive designer gear can't compete with the miracle of God's design.

> He has made everything
> beautiful in its time.
>
> ECCLESIASTES 3:11

This is perhaps my favourite beauty-related Scripture. God made you. This is your time. So that means He made you beautiful!

 Learning to see and embrace our own beauty is a process. It's not easy to forget the fairytales we've grown up with or to stop comparing ourselves with others. We need God's help to see the beauty in who we are. Let's pray!

Lord, You made everything beautiful in its time and that includes me. Help me to see my beauty. Help me reframe the way I think and feel about my appearance if I need to. Teach me to enjoy and make the most of what I have. And mostly, give me faith to believe that the people who matter will always see and appreciate my beauty, both inside and out. In Jesus' name. Amen.

Section Eight

Sex and sexuality

I'm taking a deep breath as I begin to write this section. I'm excited to delve into a subject I have passion for. I'm also nervous to go on record about something so personal and culturally sensitive. It would be far easier to leave the entire subject out of this journal. But when I picture you, the young person reading this book, I can't bring myself to ignore something that has such power to shape your life. I've been asking myself, *'What would I want my little girl to hear if she picked up a journal like this?'* So that's what you're going to get in this section.

I'll start by saying that all the following opinions are my own. I've been gathering these thoughts for more than twenty years, both from experience and study. I don't speak for any particular organisation and it's not my job (or anyone's for that matter) to tell you how to live your life. I'm not about to preach to or judge you. My heart is to stand alongside you as a sister and point you towards what you deserve. Sex is one of God's greatest gifts to humankind and there's no reason why you should settle for anything other than the best version of it.

As with the other sections of this journal, these pages are here to help you figure out what you want from *your* life and who *you* want to be. When it comes to creating the life we want, all our choices are important. Sexual choices are no different. Understanding the true beauty, power and meaning of sex has been a journey for me. As someone who started that journey as a curious, rebellious teen and wound up as a Christian abstaining from sex until marriage, I feel I've seen the picture from both angles. Although it's not easy for me to share certain parts of that picture with you, it's one hundred per cent worthwhile if it saves you heartache and steers you towards life.

This is super personal, so don't feel you have to put anything on paper if you don't want to. But this is a safe space to be honest. How do you feel about sexuality within your own life? Are you worried about what God thinks of you or your sexuality, or about what others may think? Has something happened in your life that you feel shame or confusion about? Feel free to use the following space to reflect. Remember, there is no judgement or condemnation here.

Aside from being the way babies are made (spoiler alert), sex is integral to most romantic, adult relationships. Because it's essential for the survival of our species, sexuality is wired into us biologically, physiologically and socially. It finds its way into every element of our culture, from the glistening torsos of underwear models to the lyrics of our favourite radio tunes. Sex is more than an act though. It's a part of the life-force that connects everything in the natural world. They don't call it the birds and the bees for nothing!

With sex being so central to life, you'd think we'd be awesome at discussing it, right? Unfortunately, this doesn't seem to be the case. In spite of its role within our culture and identity, daily dialogue about sex is pretty limited and the messaging we pick up from around us isn't always that helpful.

Information about sex is pretty easy to access, thanks to the internet. But not much of it teaches us how to make good choices, communicate our boundaries or deal with mistakes. If we type our sex questions into Google, we're likely to come across all sorts of stuff that focuses on the physical side. But sex is not just physical; it affects us body, mind and soul. Guidance on how to navigate the non-physical levels to sexual relationship is pretty thin on the ground. We need more open dialogue about the emotional, mental and spiritual impacts of our sexual choices. It's sad that we're more likely to find information about dealing with sexual trauma than we are about creating good experiences to begin with.

Because sex is generally private, we often feel a little embarrassed or vulnerable being open about it. But there's nothing shameful about sex in itself. Sex isn't bad. But it can be reduced to something it was never meant to be. We need to arm ourselves with knowledge and wisdom if we're going to enjoy it for all it can be.

Why should we learn about sex?

Typically, we learn about sex in stages. The first stage is usually a quick rundown about where babies come from. The next lesson tends to happen at secondary school when we get the reproduction and contraception talk. To be honest, the adult-led teaching often ends there. From that point, if we want to know more, we have to do our own research. And of course we want to know more!

In our early teens, hormones awaken our sexuality. The onset of puberty and all its mayhem sparks a sudden awareness of this new world. We might begin to wonder if we're attractive to others. Questions of 'who likes whom' and 'who is doing what with whom' might begin to arise within our peer groups. We might get the opportunity to watch pornography or even experience things for ourselves. But learning about sex from locker-room talk and pornography can be super confusing. Instead of getting answers, our heads get filled with all kinds of anxieties, false ideals and expectations. Just like beauty marketing, pornography often reinforces damaging body stereotypes, which can affect our self-image. We also might feel pressure to look and behave in certain ways sexually within relationships.

Rather than preparing us for great sex, these kinds of research often end up leaving us with more fears and hang-ups than before.

Part 2: The power and importance of good choices

First, it's important to say, the legal age of consent in the UK is sixteen. It's against the law to engage in sexual activity before this. It's also against the law to send or share sexually explicit or nude pictures of yourself or anyone else under this age. Once you reach the age of consent, your actions concerning your body are up to you. This includes when, how and with whom you are physically intimate.

But making good choices in this area is crucial for your physical, mental and spiritual health. Just because you can doesn't mean you should. Back to that great Scripture, '"Everything is permissible for me," but not everything is beneficial' (1 Cor. 6:12 BSB). Just because something is legal or socially acceptable doesn't mean it will be right for you. The decisions you make for your body affect more than just your body. Physical intimacy connects to our emotions, mind and soul. There is a tremendous vulnerability that comes with sharing your body and let's not forget, sex is supposed to be good! So it's really not worth going there unless you have a foundation of complete trust and communication.

The world would have us believe we can isolate the physical side of sex to make it more 'casual'. But engaging in something so intimate can never be casual. In order for sex to be only physical, you'd have to disconnect from your thoughts and emotions. If you have to disconnect from your thoughts and emotions to be intimate, it's probably not a great idea! Emotions aside, our biology is designed to connect during sex, with the release of powerful hormones like oxytocin, known as the *'bonding'* or *'love'* hormone. This alone can make it hard to detach from someone we've been physically intimate with.

Boundaries and consent

> Guard your heart above all else, for it determines the course of your life.
>
> PROVERBS 4:23 NLT

Consent is a hot topic right now. Far too many people have stories about traumatic or damaging sexual encounters. In an age where people are increasingly adventurous, it's important we learn how to be clear about what we do and don't want. The word 'consent' means *'permission for something to happen or agreement to do something'*. Most of us know that 'no means no'. But sometimes, saying no feels difficult or awkward. If we say yes to something because we feel obligated or under pressure, we can deeply regret what happens next. It's important we set boundaries in our hearts and confidently guard them.

For lots of us, trauma doesn't just come from being assaulted or violated. Trauma can come because we said *'yes'* when our hearts were saying *'no'* or *'I'm not sure'*. Our lives and future relationships can be seriously affected by trauma, so we have to remember that consenting with our hearts is as important as consenting with our words.

Cultural pressure

> Do not conform to the pattern of this world, but be transformed by the renewing of your mind. Then you will be able to test and approve what God's will is – his good, pleasing and perfect will.
>
> ROMANS 12:2

We've all heard about 'peer pressure' when it comes to sex and we know that pressure can come from within a relationship too. But what we talk about far less is the *cultural* pressure to have sex once we start dating. It's presumed that everyone is sleeping together and if they're not, they probably should be!

This isn't the case at all. Plenty of people decide to wait a while. Some even decide to wait until marriage, like my husband and I did. Cultural pressure is just as unacceptable as any other sort. We know it's not okay to coerce or persuade someone to do things they're not ready for. We shouldn't accept that coercion from society either. Whatever you believe, **be clear about your boundaries from the start**. Anyone who isn't willing to respect what's important to you is not worth your time and *definitely* not worth compromising for.

The thief comes only to steal and kill and destroy; I have come that they may have life, and have it to the full.

JOHN 10:10

Okay, now we get on to the good stuff. If culture, porn, school and the internet don't hold the keys to good sex, who does? That's right … God.

People seldom put God and sex in the same sentence. There's a presumption that anything relating to the spiritual must be a total passion-killer. In fact, it's totally the opposite. Embracing the spiritual dimension to your sexuality is like upgrading to the premium version of the app, getting rid of the trashy ads and bugs that make it crash constantly and installing the features it was always intended to have.

The Bible contains an entire book of what is essentially pillow talk. Song of Songs is about desire, connection, longing and passion. It tells the story of a couple who are totally into each other, anticipating physical intimacy as they approach their wedding night. The book is loaded with flirting and fantasy but there's also a strong emphasis on commitment. The words, *'I am my lover's, and my lover is mine'* appear several times, and this is significant. When God paints a picture of these 'lovers', they don't just **long** for each other, they **belong** to each other. Both sides are in for the long haul.

God's will for your life is fullness. This includes a healthy and enjoyable sex life! By healthy, I don't mean like a salad with no dressing or a sub-zero shower every day (unless that's your thing); I mean all the best things sex can be between attracted, connected and consenting adults, *and* a lot more. God really outdid Himself on the invention of sex. Not only did He invent desire and pleasure, He designed the biological processes to deepen relationships and create life at the same time. It's all pretty genius.

Great sex is about partnership. With the right person, sex has benefits for body, mind and soul. Studies have shown it can improve mental health, boost your immune system and improve sleep. Physical intimacy with someone you trust can even help build body confidence! A foundation of trust and respect means that instead of wondering if you're good enough, you can be uninhibited, playful, spiritual, emotional and/or all of the above. The freedom you can have with a partner who knows and loves you means sex can get better and better with time too.

The really amazing thing about God's version of sex is that it goes beyond the moment and enriches our lives as a whole. The Creator intended physical intimacy to be one of the building blocks for long-term partnership and family, not just relationally but chemically too. That release of oxytocin with the *right* person is incredibly positive, as it strengthens your bond and commitment to each other. Strong relationships have a positive effect on the people in your world, so everyone's a winner. And not forgetting, sex can literally create new life! When making love to your best friend results in the miracle of a pregnancy, it's about the best feeling there is. God's version of sex is not just about momentary pleasure or curiosity. It's about wellness, confidence, connection, stability and ultimately family life.

The downgrade

The world sells us a 'fast food' version of all the good stuff above. Fast food sells itself as something just as tasty but with less effort and commitment. We kind of know it won't be as good for us but it's a cheap and convenient fix for our hunger. But as much as it's a thrill to sink our teeth into a burger moments after ordering, it doesn't usually make us feel all that great. It certainly can't compare to a Michelin-star restaurant experience, steeped in romance, flavour, flare and goodness. Casual sex is a bit like fast food. It often seems like a good idea at the time, a quick fix for our appetite, emptiness or boredom. But it can leave us feeling pretty crumby afterwards.

Casual sex can have a number of disappointing outcomes. For one, it can leave us feeling lonely. Having that momentary connection with someone might 'fill us up' temporarily. But the emptiness that often follows is no fun at all. If alcohol is involved it can add to the confusion and regret further. 'Hook up' culture is extremely messy and 'no strings' sex is usually anything but. Aside from the obvious pitfalls like the potential for unwanted pregnancy and STIs, unappealing baggage like insecurity, embarrassment, jealousy and, yes, quite often underwhelming/awkward sex often comes along with it. Another issue can be uncertainty about the status of your relationship. When you've been physically intimate with someone but don't have any clue where it's going, it can create all kinds of confusion and even heartache.

The bottom line is, you're worth more. God doesn't want something as incredible as sex to leave you feeling empty, used, humiliated, confused or lonely. He doesn't want you to share the most intimate parts of yourself with someone who isn't committed to you and your enjoyment, or become attached to someone who isn't right for you. You're far too precious.

God wants you to have the five-star experience. He knows you're worth a partner who will put you first sexually and in life too. He knows that the right partner will bring out the best in you, move you confidently in the direction of your dreams and honour your body.

You may have to work a little harder and wait a little longer for that. But just like that gourmet meal, it will be worth the investment!

Sexuality identity

Sexuality is one dimension of who we are. If you like, it's a single facet to the jewel of how we identify. It was never meant to be shrouded in shame or handled recklessly by others. As it goes, this facet of the jewel is a very personal one. It was never intended to be a political 'hot topic'; never intended to be used as a weapon or as a tool for propaganda. Your sexuality is **potent**, it's **powerful** and it's **yours**. You're on a journey and you are more than a political conversation.

A few months ago, a young person sent me a message via social media. She told me she was a young Christian struggling with her sexuality and wondered what she should do. I said that, honestly, something as personal as her sexuality was not for me to comment on. Someone like me, who doesn't know her, shouldn't be speaking into her journey to any degree that could hurt or confuse her. Anyone who does speak into her sexuality should be someone of her choosing, who is willing to walk that journey with her.

Having said that, I believe that what I've shared in this section applies universally. Your body matters, your heart matters and you deserve a partner who will put you first, even if you have to wait a while to find them. The worst outcome in my view would be to let your sexuality or what anyone else says about it come between you and Jesus. Sometimes people, even with the greatest of intentions, are insensitive and cruel. Jesus loves you enough to die for you however you identify. He will never turn you away or love you any less.

Reflect and Reframe

Why not take a few minutes to decide what you want for your life when it comes to sex and relationships. What are important boundaries for you? What would your dream partner need to honour in you?

Write some thoughts below.

....

....

....

....

....

....

....

....

....

Part 4:
Redemption

> This means that anyone who belongs to Christ has become a new person. The old life is gone; a new life has begun!
>
> 2 CORINTHIANS 5:17 NLT

As we close this section, there is one last thing I want to share with you: God's power to bring us healing and redemption. As I said in the beginning, I've had a journey of my own. I've experienced the transforming power of God's redeeming love. Because so much of what we've covered in this section could be triggering, I thought it only right I share a bit of my own story so you know you're not alone.

I've always wanted to be liked. I guess we all do. But that got more intense when I started secondary school. I didn't know anyone to begin  with so it became really important to me to 'fit in'. By age fourteen, I remember feeling a lot older in my head than I actually was. I started partying with older friends and dressed myself to look older so I could get into night clubs (without my parents' permission). I never saw myself as attractive so didn't expect to gain attention from men, but I did. Because I passed for eighteen, I ended up hooking up with older guys on nights out. I felt in control and happy, just dancing and meeting people. But one night didn't go to plan. I went to a house party with a couple of friends and ended up alone with a guy twice my age. Because he thought I was older than I was, I remember feeling pressure to do what he expected of me. I tried to hint in all sorts of ways that I wasn't really up for anything but he persisted and things went too far. In hindsight what took place wasn't consensual.

I didn't realise at the time what an impact this had had on me. The overwhelming feeling I had was regret and shame at my 'stupidity'. Because I shouldn't have been out at all, I felt as though what had happened was entirely my fault. I felt I'd let myself down and was angry with myself for not being clearer with this man about how I felt. Deep down I knew I'd thrown something special away. From that point onwards, I really didn't have good boundaries at all. I felt that my innocence had gone so it really didn't matter what happened afterwards. In some ways, doing whatever I wanted was my way of regaining control and feeling more positive about sex.

They say you accept the love you feel you deserve. That's pretty much where the story went next for me. Over the years that followed, I was in and out of relationships, unable to feel secure and becoming increasingly depressed.

In 2004, I met some Christians through an open mic night I helped to host. After getting to know them a little, I went along with them to a small Christian music event. Following the initial awkwardness of staring at song lyrics projected onto a wall, I started to feel something happening. It was a little scary but I felt the strongest urge to pray. I'd heard my Christian friends talk about being a 'new creation' in Jesus. I felt so tired and so messed up, I was finally willing to lay down my life and start again. So that's what I did. I asked God to help me start my life over and I felt a weight had been lifted from my shoulders immediately. Over the days that followed, I sensed the shadows were moving and the light was coming in. I knew that God had removed the baggage from my past and I'd been given a clean slate. Over the next months, I could feel myself healing from the past. I no longer felt I was carrying what had happened to me when I was younger. It was completely incredible. Miraculous even. From that time onwards, I promised myself I would treat my body as though it was something to be valued.

So then I met Joel ... a year younger than I was and a pastor's son. He was different from anyone I'd dated before. I was reluctant to start dating him at first because he was so 'untouched'. Because of his strong church upbringing, he also wanted to wait for his wife before having sex and had never dated before. When he took me out on that first date he told me straight—he thought I was that woman. It was kind of awkward for a minute. Even though I'd started a new life, I still felt I had a 'past' he deserved to know about. I thought a guy like Joel deserved someone a little cleaner cut than I was. When I tried to warn him that I was new to faith and may not be quite as 'perfect' as he was, he smiled. 'I think you're a great girl of God,' he said. He seemed to grasp better than I did that **the past is the past**.

And so we started our journey. We were different in so many ways. But in the things that mattered we were on the same page. We both wanted a life of adventure, centred around our faith. We both lived for music too (he's a drummer). And we both wanted to have sex for the first time on our wedding night. We dated for four years. Four years of saying goodbye with a kiss on the doorstep. Four years of avoiding sleeping in the same room, even when it would have been more convenient to. In September 2009 we had our perfect day. We gave our lives to each other and then our bodies.

Our wedding night was more emotional than I thought it would be. Caught up in the fun of the day, it was hard to imagine what the bridal suite had in store for us. But it was every bit as magical as you would hope. We had made it. It felt like we'd gone the distance, built the framework for something awesome and paid the price for each other. As we spent those first moments of intimacy together, I knew the final piece of my healing was taking place. What was taken from me all those years ago was restored.

As I mentioned earlier, Joel and I have been married almost twelve years now. We've had our ups and downs and it isn't always perfect. But our relationship gets better every day and I'm so grateful for what we have. We've travelled the world together and had so many adventures. We've faced challenges of course, but our faith gets us through. I thank God all the time that we gave our dating years to Him. A lot of people think of a wedding as the 'cherry on the cake' of their journey together. For us it was day one of our adventure. I think it set us up for the calling we have and the life we lead. We had our first child this year.

I asked Joel why it was important for him that we waited. He said: 'I'd prayed for God to help me find the one to spend my life with. That person was you. I wanted us to set a good example for others and one day for our own children.'

Your story will be different to the one you've just read. I don't want you to compare your experiences or your relationships to mine. But I hope you realise that whatever you've been through and whatever you believe, it's always possible to find healing and start over. You don't have to carry your past or feel like damaged goods. God's love restores.

However you feel about this section, perhaps it's given you something to think about. Again, please remember these thoughts and beliefs are my own. But I hope the words have helped you figure out what you want from your relationships, and inspired you not to settle for less than you're worth. Let's have a pray …

Lord, thank You for Your redeeming love. Thank You that it's never too late to start over and, in You, we can be made fully new. Thank You for the healing and restoration that can be found in Your arms. And, Lord, help me to honour my body and live in my true worth, reflected on the cross. Amen.

Section Nine

Experiences past, present and future

> You are the sum total of everything you've ever seen, heard, eaten, smelled, been told, forgot—it's all there. Everything influences each of us, and because of that I try to make sure that my experiences are positive.[6]
>
> MAYA ANGELOU

This final section of the journal is about our experiences. What we experience in life has a huge impact on who we become. One of the reasons each person is completely unique is we have all experienced different things. Even those within our own families have completely different experiences to us.

The Maya Angelou quote is very true. We *are* shaped by the people we meet, the places we go, things we see, taste and hear etc. But unfortunately, not all our experiences can be positive or enjoyable. Some of the things we go through in life are tough. We might even feel we'd rather forget them. This section is about making the most of our experiences and using them to shape us into something better.

Honesty First

Let's take a few moments now to be honest about our experiences and how they might have shaped who we are.

My past has been ...
Try to write something about your past and how it has shaped you. Perhaps find one positive and one negative thing.

My present is ...

Try to write a little about what you're going through right now and how it might be shaping you.

....

....

....

....

....

....

....

My future will be ...

Try to imagine what your future might be like and how the past might shape it.

....

....

....

....

....

....

....

being confident of this, that he who began a good work in you will carry it on to completion until the day of Christ Jesus.

PHILIPPIANS 1:6

If you've had a difficult time or you're struggling right now, you might find it hard to look to the future. If the home you grew up in was chaotic, you might

not be looking forward to marriage or family life. If you struggled in education, you might be worried about finding a career you enjoy. If you've suffered a lot of grief or loss, you might be carrying that with you right now. But it's important to remember, **even though your past informs your future, it doesn't have to define it**! If you started life in an unhappy home, it doesn't mean you're doomed to create one. If you had a hard time at school, it doesn't mean you won't have a meaningful and enjoyable career.

It's helpful to think of your life as a story God is writing. Just like any good story it has a beginning, a middle and an ending. No matter how your story begins or the troubles you face, God can work in and through it all to give you a bright, brilliant ending. Somehow, when we give our lives to Him, He's able to gather up the pieces and make sense of everything.

GOD CAN USE YOUR PAST TO COMFORT OTHERS

Praise be to the God and Father of our Lord Jesus Christ, the Father of compassion and the God of all comfort, who comforts us in all our troubles, so that we can comfort those in any trouble with the comfort we ourselves receive from God.

2 CORINTHIANS 1:3–4

When I found faith at age twenty, I was kind of in a mess. Not much in my life made any sense. I remember wondering, *'Why is all this happening to me?'* Then one day, I opened my New Testament at this Scripture from Corinthians and it spoke straight to my soul! I realised that someday God was going to use what I'd been through to help someone else. And just look, I'm sharing it with you right now! If you allow it, something you've struggled with can be the key to someone else's freedom or breakthrough.

GOD CAN USE YOUR CURRENT STRUGGLE TO BLESS YOUR FUTURE

but we also glory in our sufferings, because we know that suffering produces perseverance; perseverance, character; and character, hope.

ROMANS 5:3–4

Character is far more important than brains, talent, money, status or fame. Why? Because without strong character, you're unlikely to hang on to any of those other things for long. If you have a bunch of talent but a weak character, you'll become easily discouraged and insecure. If you win the lottery jackpot tomorrow but haven't done any work on your character, you're likely to fritter it all away pretty quickly. Character is an incredible asset. And since suffering has the ability to produce character, we should do our best to milk it for all it's worth.

The Bible says suffering produces character if we're willing to persevere. In other words, if we quit during a testing season or become bitter and discouraged, we might never turn it around. But if we push through in tough times, the experience can leave us stronger, wiser and armed with hope for the future. So, if you're going through something horrendous right now, don't despair. I'm not suggesting you should dance around happily about every horrible thing that happens; that's not realistic. But if you're willing to stare your hard times in the face and say, *'I'm going to rinse every last bit of goodness out of this'*, you can come out of the situation better than before. God can use your test to build a testimony. He can build your spiritual muscle so that the next battle doesn't feel so tough.

GOD DOESN'T WASTE ANYTHING

And we know that in all things God works for the good of those who love him, who have been called according to his purpose.

ROMANS 8:28

Sometimes things don't work out the way we plan. We may have some failures in our past. We might have failed in a job or a subject we were studying. We might have failed relationships or have aimed for things we didn't win. Just know, God is able to use it all. Failed experiments give us all kinds of data about what to try next. Every failed attempt at something shows us one more way not to do it. Messing up doesn't have to mean you take a dozen steps back. In fact, it can be a step forward.

This is why '*Reframing*' can be so useful and so important. If we're willing to take our experiences, find the positives and move forward, we can make use of everything, just like God does.

Take a look back at those notes about your experiences in life. Try to reframe what you've written to be even more positive. For example, if you've written about something horrible you've been through, perhaps begin to imagine how that experience could help someone else when you're feeling stronger.

Lord, thank You for my life. Thank You for the things I've done, seen and been through. It hasn't all been easy, but because You're such a good and creative God, I know You can use it to build others, build my character and help me build a good future. I know You have good plans for me and I'm choosing to embrace them today in Jesus' name. Amen.

Section Ten

Pulling it all together

We're finally coming to the end of the journal! Well done for making it through. I really hope it's helped you to paint a clearer picture in your mind of who you are in God and where you want to go. In the end, living by faith allows every day to be a new day and for us to have hope for the future. It's really all about reframing the negatives, reaching for thoughts, habits and people who give us life, and embracing our God-given identity. All things are possible in Him! And remember, God loves you enough to die for you. You're worthy of a full and beautiful life, so don't settle for anything less.

> Definition of **manifesto**: a written statement declaring publicly the intentions, motives, or views of its issuer.

For this penultimate exercise, we're going to pull out some of the key things from the journal to write ourselves a manifesto. Hopefully, this will help create an overview of the things we've learned about who we are in God and who we are going to become by His grace. It's kind of like writing a mission statement for life. Just write a couple of lines under each heading.

I hope that reading it back will fill you with purpose and confidence!

After filling in the blanks on the following pages, take your manifesto off the page and write it somewhere else. Type it up and print it out or draw and doodle it decoratively onto paper. Get creative. Or don't. The beauty of all this is it's entirely up to you. This is your one precious life. Grab it, live it and love it.

My personal manifesto/mission statement

My name is …

....

I believe that God is …

....

....

....

I believe that I am …

....

....

....

I believe that others are …

....

....

....

My core values are …

My strengths, abilities and talents are …

My passions are …

My purpose in life is …

I'm beautiful because ...

My ideal life partner will have these qualities ...

My boundaries within relationships are ...

My past is ...

I'm enjoying the following about my present …

My future will be …

A final look at who we are

> I press on towards the goal to win the prize for which God has called me heavenwards in Christ Jesus.
>
> PHILIPPIANS 3:14

Finally, precious reader, let's revisit the first exercise of this journal. Hopefully you'll find that this process has improved your sense of identity. Don't worry if you still have work to do; we all have room to grow and always will. Perhaps come back in six months and do the exercise again when you've had more of a chance to put words into practice.

Do you feel you know who you are?

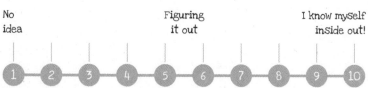

No idea — Figuring it out — I know myself inside out!

1 2 3 4 5 6 7 8 9 10

How do you feel about yourself in general?

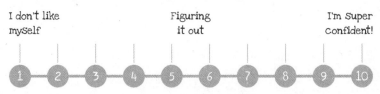

How do you feel about your physical appearance?

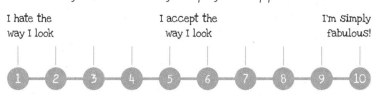

How do you feel about your future?

What about your gifts and talents?

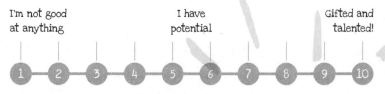

And how are the relationships in your life?

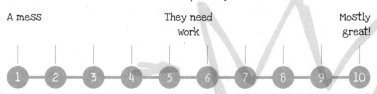

 *Endnotes*

1 https://www.lexico.com/definition/identity

2 https://www.news.ucsb.edu/2009/012739/ucsb-philosopher-examines-reasonable-disagreement-and-political-policy

3 Credited to Bernard Meltzer from his call-in radio programme in the United States which ran from 1967

4 Aesop (2015), *Aesop's Fables*, p.109, Sheba Blake Publishing

5 Dahl, R (2016), *The Twits*, (London: Penguin Books)

6 Interview from the April 2011 edition of *O, The Oprah Magazine*